Anita Reith Stohs

Praise God with Shapes

Circles, Triangles, Squares, and More!

Patterns and Diagrams by Susan Morris

CONCORDIA PUBLISHING HOUSE · SAINT LOUIS

To Abbie and Jakob Versemann, 2 Timothy 3:14–15

3558 S. Jefferson Ave., St. Louis, MO 63118-3968
1-800-325-3040 • www.cph.org

Manufactured in the United States of America

2 3 4 5 6 7 8 9 10 21 20 19 18 17 16 15 14 13

Contents

Introduction

God uses a variety of shapes in His wonderful creation. Encourage the children in your class to look around to find some of the many ways God uses shapes to add variety and beauty. Check out books on nature from the library to show children the myriad ways in which we can see God's creativity in our world.

This book provides a connection between the shapes in our world and the story of God's love for us. It uses simple shapes as patterns for a variety of easy-to-make craft projects that reinforce familiar Bible stories and passages. Use the shapes alone or in combination to provide a variety of fun, creative activities for classroom or home.

As much as possible, encourage children to look for and trace items in the classroom as patterns for the shapes they need to complete the projects. If this is not possible, use the pattern pieces provided. Enlarge or reduce patterns with a photocopy machine or overhead projector. Or allow children who are able to draw and cut their own patterns themselves.

Although these activities are intended for use with children in kindergarten through second grade, they can also be adapted for use with younger children or older students with developmental disabilities. Older children may even wish to adapt the projects to make banners.

Creativity is a special gift from God. Its expression through art can be viewed as an act of praise, much like singing or playing an instrument. May this book be a springboard for you and your students as you explore the many ways to praise God using the shapes He Himself created in our world.

Anita Stohs

Circle Patterns

Stick Puppet

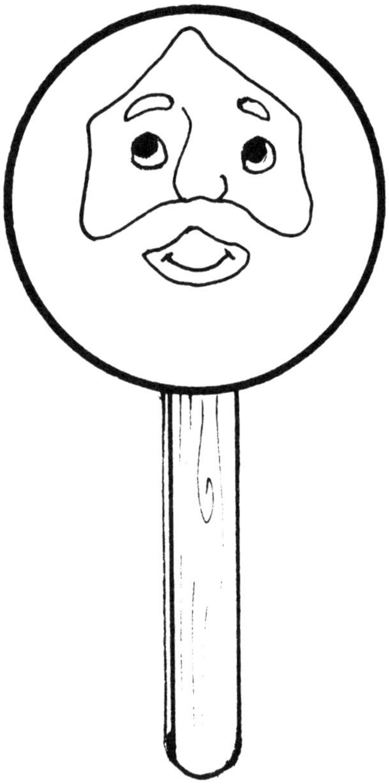

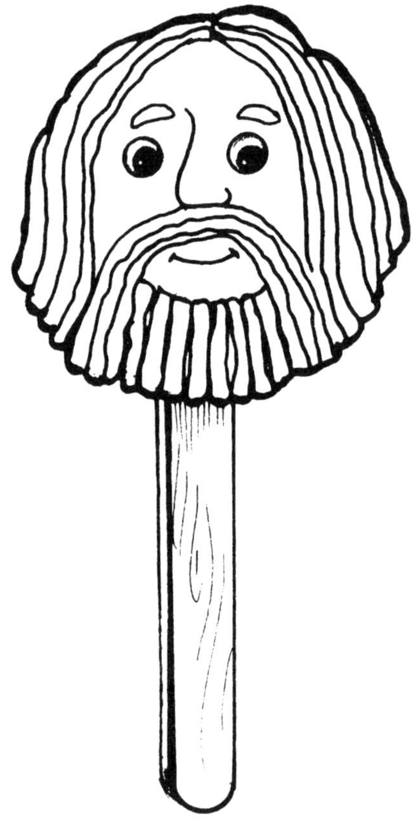

What You Need

Construction paper
(use colors representing a variety of skin tones)
Craft stick
Markers, crayons, or colored pencils
Scissors
Pencil
Glue

What You Do

1. Use any of the circles on page 5 as a pattern, or trace a circle-shaped object found in your classroom.
2. Draw a face on the circle.
3. Glue the circle to the end of a craft stick.

More to Do

1. Color faces with crayons in multiracial colors.
2. Glue on movable craft eyes and yarn hair.

The Lesson Connection

The Great Commission: Matthew 28:16–20

Make a puppet face to represent Jesus, then use it to tell the story of the Great Commission. Have the children make puppets representing themselves. Ask them to take turns using their puppets to show how they might tell someone else the Good News that Jesus died on the cross and rose again for the forgiveness of our sins. Then suggest that children take the puppets home and share this Good News with their families and friends.

Grapes

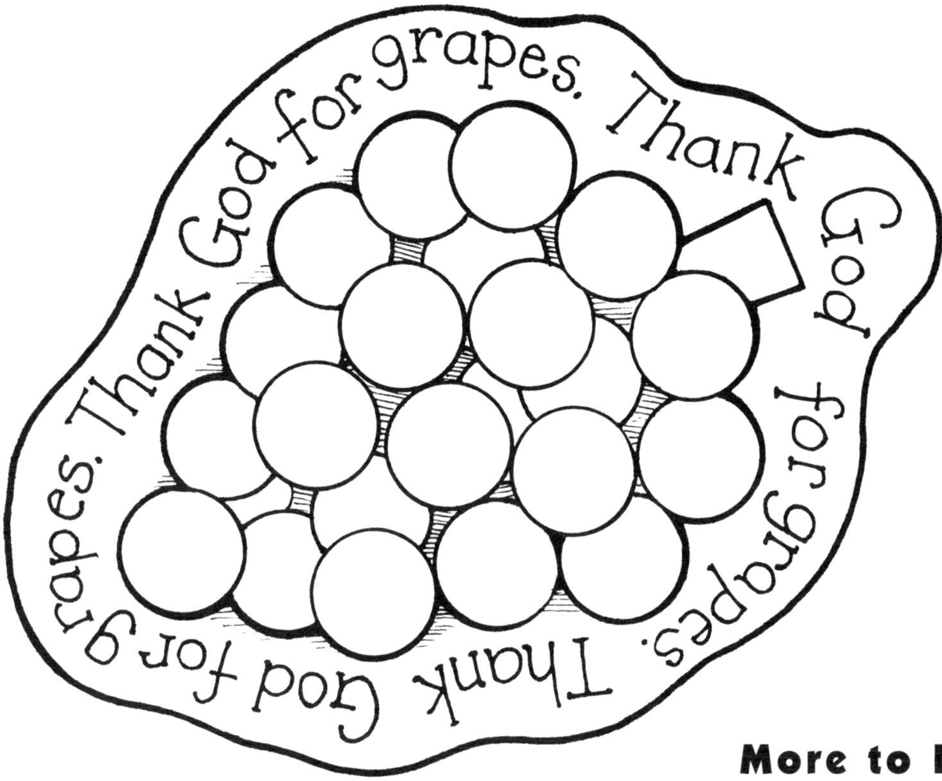

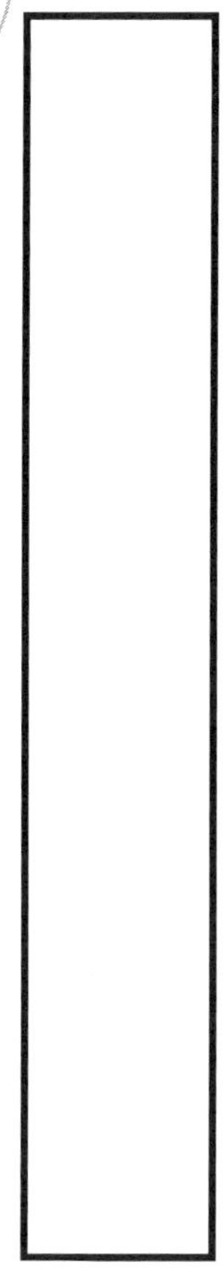

What You Need

Purple and green construction paper
Scissors
Glue
Pencil

What You Do

1. Using a circle pattern from page 5 or a round object found in your room, trace several circles onto purple construction paper and cut them out.
2. Glue purple circles together to make a bunch of grapes.
3. Cut a narrow green rectangle and glue it to the top of the bunch of grapes as a stem. (Use the optional pattern given.)

More to Do

1. Glue the bunch of grapes onto a sheet of paper and add a Bible verse or religious saying.
2. Glue the grapes to a sheet of paper and cut a ½" margin around them, then write the phrase "Thank God for Grapes" around it, separating each word with a dot.
3. Cut small grapes from craft foam and glue them together to form a bunch. Attach a magnet to the back to make a refrigerator magnet.
4. Stick gummed stickers together to make a bunch of grapes.

The Lesson Connection

God Created Food: Genesis 2:9

Make a bunch of grapes as a reminder that God created the food we eat. As the children work, have them think of other foods that are round. Invite the children to say a prayer thanking God for these gifts of food.

Flowers and Vase

What You Need

Construction paper
Pencil
Scissors

What You Do

1. Using the patterns on page 5, trace and cut an equal number of large and small circles, plus one half-circle.
2. If desired, fringe the outside of the large circles for petals.
3. Glue a small circle to the center of a large circle.
4. Cut strips of green paper to represent stems. For leaves, cut ovals (pattern on page 11) or triangles (pattern on page 23).
5. Glue each flower to a stem. Add leaves.
6. Fold half-circle into a cone and glue the straight sides together to make a vase. Glue the flowers inside it.

More to Do

1. Cut the flowers from wrapping paper, wallpaper, decorative paper, or craft foam sheets.
2. Write an appropriate phrase or verse onto the cone with a fine-tip marker.
3. Glue flowers onto craft sticks or chenille sticks (use craft glue).
4. Omit cone vase and glue flowers onto a piece of paper to make a poster.
5. Make small flowers and glue to a piece of paper to make stationery.
6. Make different kinds of flowers by cutting circles in half or by tracing different sizes of circles.
7. Use colored circle stickers or large sequins for flower centers.

The Lesson Connection

God Cares for Us: Luke 12:27–31

As the children make their flowers, discuss ways God cares for flowers. Expand this into a discussion of how God cares for us. Explain that the most important way God cares for us is through our Savior, Jesus Christ. Write "God Cares for You" on the vase, add the flowers, and give it to a special someone.

Dayspring

What You Need

Construction paper
Crayons, markers, or colored pencils
Pencil
Scissors
Hole punch
Yarn or string

What You Do

1. Use as a pattern the large circle on page 5. As an option, trace a large circle found in your room.
2. Trace and cut a circle. Starting at the outside edge, draw a spiral inside the circle, leaving space at the center for attaching yarn as a hanger.
3. Decorate the inside of the spiral with words, pictures, shapes, designs, sequins, or stickers.
4. Cut along the spiral.
5. Punch a hole at one end of the spiral and attach a piece of yarn for a hanger.

More to Do

1. Cut the circle from wrapping or other decorative paper.
2. Cut small "dayspring" from metallic or craft paper.
3. Decorate both sides of the spiral.

The Lesson Connection

Creation of the Heavens: Genesis 1:14–19

Cut a circle from dark blue or black construction paper. Use white crayons, or crayons designed for use on construction paper, to draw stars, comets, planets, the sun, and the earth; or add star stickers. As you work, invite the children to talk about the many beautiful objects God has placed in His heavens. Ask them to think about God's most amazing creation: His children!

Rainbow

What You Need

Construction paper
Markers or crayons
Hole punch
Yarn
Scissors
Pencil

What You Do

1. Use as a pattern the half-circle on this page. Or trace and cut a circle from the patterns on page 5 or from one found in your classroom; then fold the circle in half and cut a half-circle.
2. Starting at the outside top of the half-circle, color in stripes of color, leaving a small half circle uncolored at the center.
3. Cut the white center of the half-circle away or write an appropriate religious message in the space.
4. Punch a hole at the top of the rainbow and tie a piece of yarn through it for hanging.

More to Do

1. Cut or tear small pieces of paper in appropriate colors and glue them to the rainbow.
2. Make a stand-up rainbow. Fold a circle in half, color a rainbow on the top half, add appropriate words or picture at the center, then stand the rainbow with the bottom of the circle folded back as a base.

The Lesson Connection

God Saves Noah and His Family: Genesis 9:15–22

Glue the rainbow onto a larger piece of paper. Draw the ark in the space under the rainbow, or add the words "God Keeps His Promises." As you work, talk about Bible stories that tell how God kept His many promises to His people. Expand into a discussion of the many promises He keeps in our lives today.

Oval Patterns

Mask

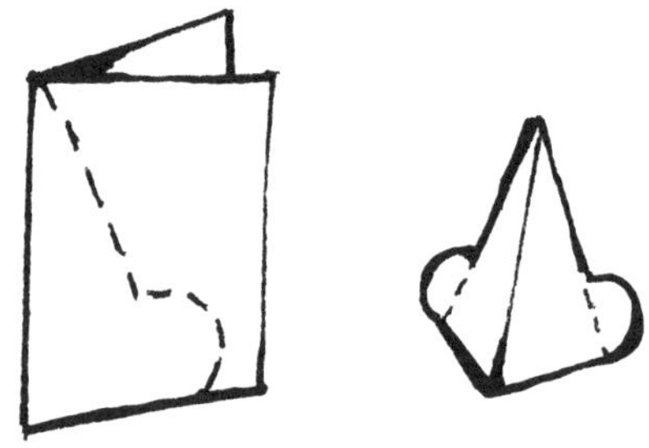

Step 5

What You Need

Construction paper or poster board
Crayons, markers, or colored pencils
Jumbo craft sticks
Glue or tape
Pencil
Scissors

What You Do

1. Use as patterns the large and small ovals on page 11.
2. Cut a large oval for an adult mask and a small oval for a child mask.
3. Color in facial features.
4. Glue or tape the oval to a jumbo craft stick.
5. Hold up masks as you act out a Bible story.

More to Do

1. Cut circles for eyes and a half-circle for the mouth.
2. Glue on gummed circles or movable craft eyes. Add yarn for hair, or "curl" strips of construction paper by pulling the strip between your finger and a *dull* scissors edge.
3. Cut holes for eyes, attach an elastic cord, then wear the mask as you act out a story.
4. Large masks can be taped to a dowel or glued to a cardboard tube.
5. Make a 3-D nose: fold a rectangle, then cut diagonally from an outside corner to the opposite corner on the fold so you have a triangle. Unfold the nose, fold up two corners to make nostrils, and glue the nose onto the mask.

The Lesson Connection

Jesus and the Children: Mark 10:13–16

Make masks to represent key characters in the story of Jesus and the children: Jesus, a disciple, a mother, and children. As you work, ask the children how they feel knowing that Jesus also loves children today. Remind the children that Jesus came to save us from sin and to give us eternal life. Have children hold their masks as they act out the story.

Easter Egg

What You Need

White drawing or water color paper
Pencil
Scissors
White crayon
Watercolor paints
Paint brush and water
Glue and cardboard (optional)

What You Do

1. Use as a pattern a larger oval on page 11.
2. Trace and cut an oval.
3. Use a white crayon to decorate the Easter egg. Press hard.
4. Brush watercolor paint over the egg.
5. Optional: glue the sheet of paper to a piece of cardboard before painting. When the paint is dry, cut out the egg.

More to Do

1. Cut egg shapes from construction paper. Add decorative craft trim and stickers or draw designs with crayons.
2. Decorate eggs with different colors of markers.
3. Instead of using a white crayon, "draw" on the egg with white glue.
4. Cut along crayon lines to make a puzzle.

The Lesson Connection

Easter: John 20:1–18

Make an egg to celebrate Jesus' resurrection. As you work, explain how the egg is an Easter symbol for new life. When birds hatch from eggs, Christians are reminded that Jesus rose from the grave to give us new life. Put the children's eggs on a classroom bulletin board under the heading "Jesus Lives!"

Baby in a Basket

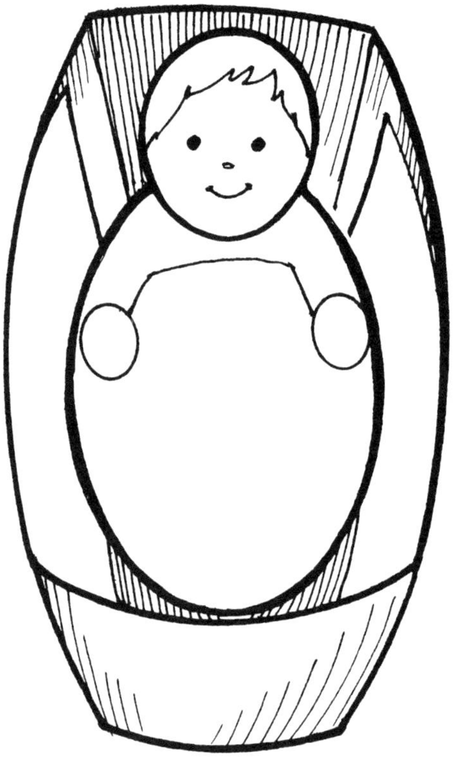

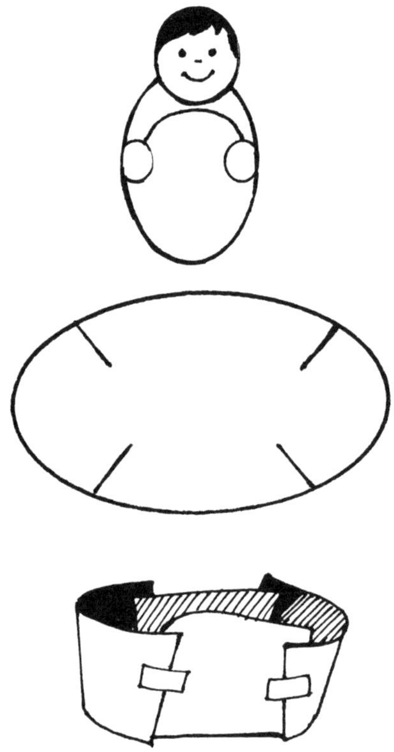

What You Need

Construction paper
Pencil
Scissors
Tape or glue
Markers, crayons, or colored pencils

What You Do

1. Use the two ovals on this page as patterns for the baby. Use the large oval on page 11 for the basket.
2. Trace and cut one of each size oval. Glue the baby's head onto the body. Color details for the baby's face and body.
3. Cut four slits into the sides of the large oval as shown in the diagram.
4. Overlap the slits and tape or glue them together to make a basket.

More to Do

1. Cut the baby's body or the basket from felt, stiff fabric, wallpaper, wrapping paper, or craft foam sheets.
2. Glue on acrylic craft hair or yarn for the baby's hair.

The Lesson Connection

Baby Moses in the Basket: Exodus 2:1–10

Use the baby and basket as a visual aid for telling the story of how God kept Moses safe in his basket-boat. Have children make a baby and basket to take home. Write "God Keeps Us Safe" on the basket. Explain to the children that everyone in God's family is a part of His plan and that He watches over and cares for us all.

Butterfly

What You Need

Construction paper
Pencil
Scissors
Crayons, markers, or colored pencils

What You Do

1. Use as patterns the ovals on this page.
2. Cut one long oval for the butterfly's body. Cut two sets of large and small ovals for the wings. Cut a small oval for the head. In addition, cut two thin strips for antennae.
3. Glue the wings onto the butterfly's body. Color details on the wings.
4. Glue the antennae strips onto the butterfly head. Include a smile and two eyes on the butterfly head.

More to Do

1. Glue or draw different shapes onto the butterfly wings for decoration, or add circle stickers.
2. Cut butterfly shapes from craft foam sheets. Use craft glue to fasten them together. Glue decorative craft trim on the wings.
3. Use a hole punch to make a hole at the top of the butterfly and tie a piece of yarn through it for hanging.
4. Make the butterfly from different-sized heart shapes (patterns on page 17).
5. Glue on movable craft eyes and pipe cleaner antennae.

The Lesson Connection

He Is Risen!: Luke 24:1–12

Review how the butterfly emerges from a dead-looking cocoon to new life. Tie this to Jesus, who died on the cross for our sins and rose again the first Easter, emerging from death to New Life. Write "He Lives" across the butterfly body; decorate the wings.

Movement Figure

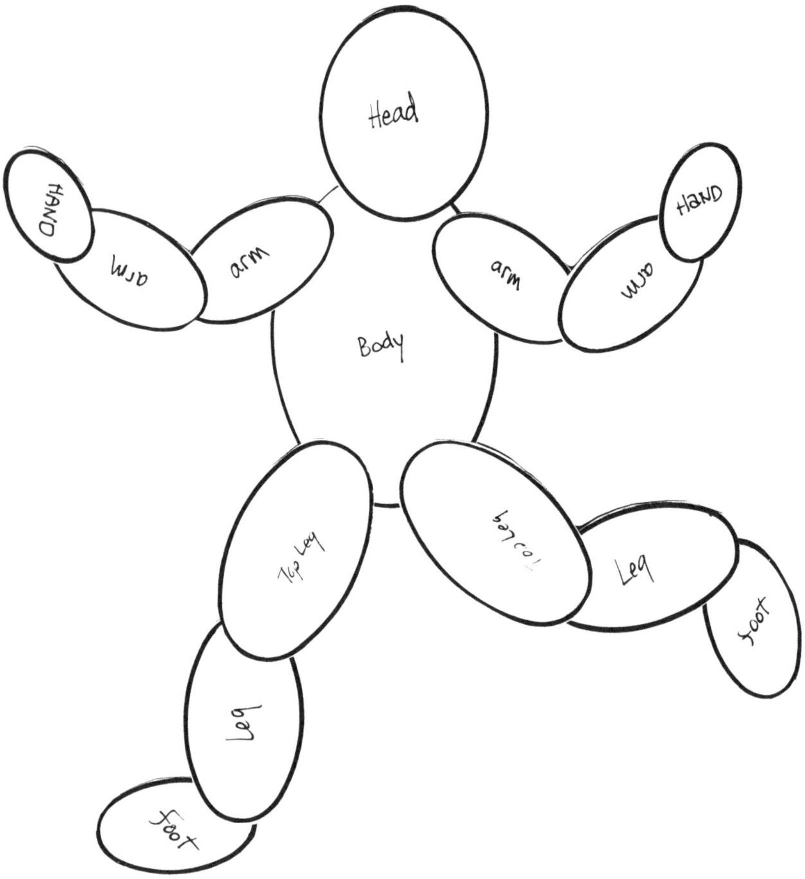

What You Need

Construction paper
Pencil
Scissors
Markers, crayons, or colored pencils (optional)

What You Do

1. Use as patterns the oval shapes on this page.
2. Trace and cut the oval shapes.
3. Fit and glue the pieces together to make a moving figure.

More to Do

1. Glue the figure onto a piece of paper. Add an appropriate saying, Bible verse, or the words "Praise the Lord."
2. Cut shapes from craft foam; glue together with tacky glue.

The Lesson Connection

Peter Heals a Crippled Man: Acts 3:1–10

Have the children fit the ovals together to show the happy man jumping for joy after he was healed. As an application, have each child make a jumping figure of him- or herself to add to a bulletin board thanking God for our bodies that are able to move in so many ways. Encourage the children to talk about the different ways they can use their bodies to praise the Lord.

Heart Patterns

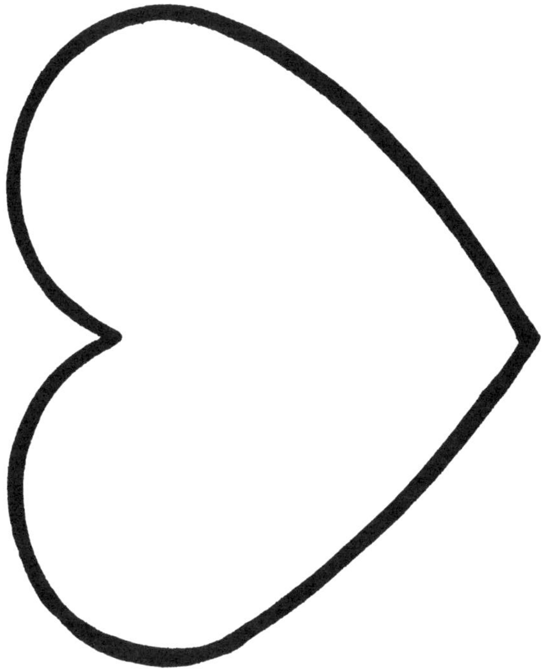

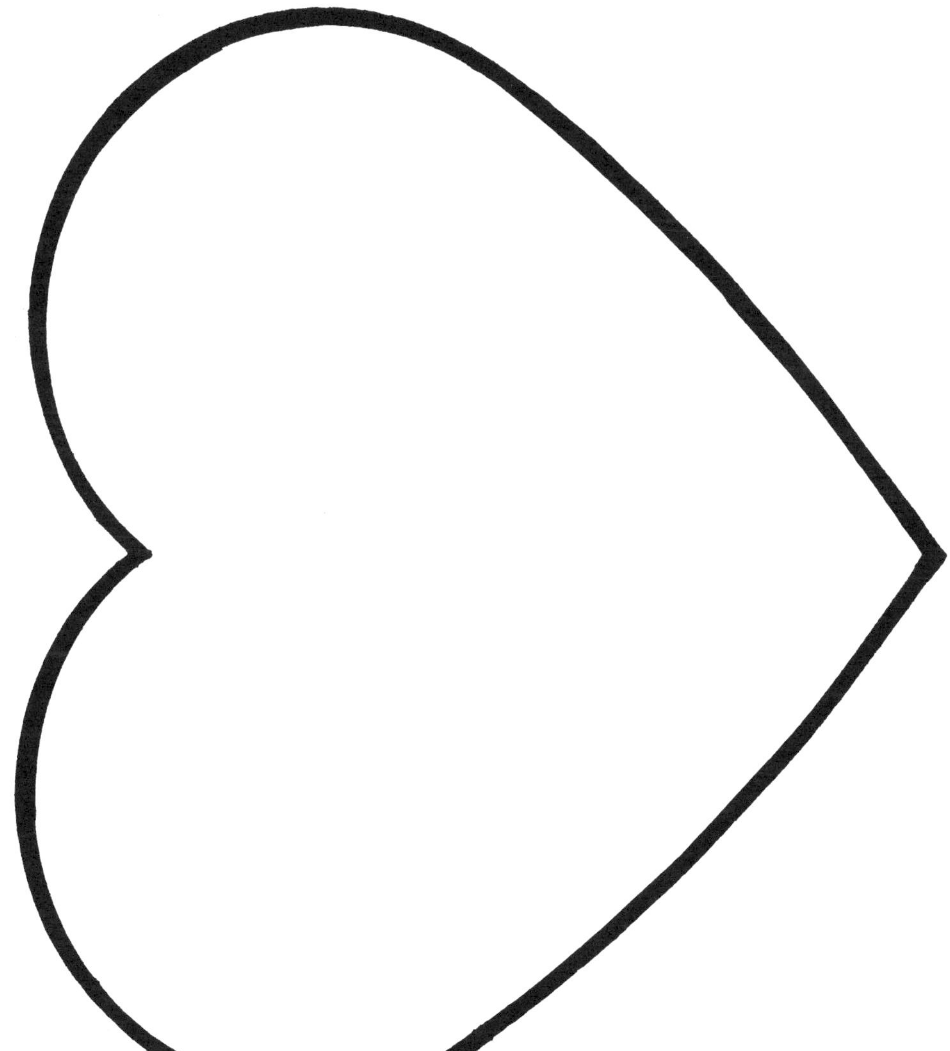

Wreath

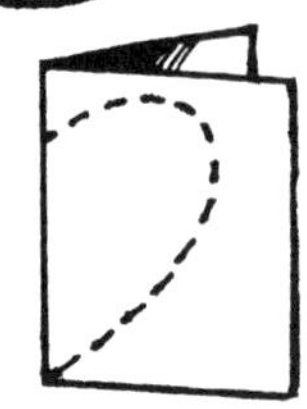

What You Need

Construction paper
Ribbon
Fine-tip marker
Glue
Pencil
Scissors

What You Do

1. Use a heart pattern provided on page 17 to trace and cut hearts. Or cut hearts from folded paper (see diagram).
2. Use one color or a variety of colors of construction paper.
3. Glue the hearts end-to-end or side-to-side to form a circle.
4. Cut a piece of ribbon, tie a bow, and glue it onto the top of the wreath.

More to Do

1. Glue decorative trim or sequins onto the hearts.
2. Cut hearts from craft foam sheets and use craft glue to glue them together.
3. Cut the rim from a paper plate; glue the hearts around it.

The Lesson Connection

The Forgiving Father: Luke 15:11–32

A heart wreath can be an excellent reminder that God loves and forgives us, His children. Use a fine-tip marker to write, "God Is Love" onto a heart cut from a different color and glue it to the bottom of the wreath. As they work, ask children to tell the story of the prodigal son in their own words. Discuss how God's love is like a circle: it is never-ending, encircling us with forgiveness, grace, and compassion.

Puppet

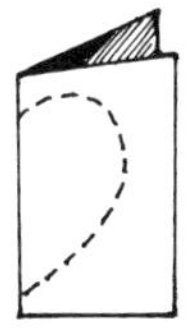

What You Need

Sturdy or stiff paper
Yarn
Jumbo craft stick
Crayon or fine-tip marker
Scissors
Glue to tape
Pencil

What You Do

1. Use heart patterns on page 17, or cut your own hearts from a piece of folded paper (see diagram).
2. Cut one large and four small hearts.
3. Draw a face onto the large heart.
4. Arrange the puppet pieces, face down, on your work area.
5. Cut four short pieces of yarn to connect the hands and feet to the puppet. Cut a longer piece of yarn to connect the body to the craft stick. Cut two longer pieces of yarn to connect the hands to the craft stick. (See the illustration of the finished puppet.)
6. Glue or tape the yarn to the puppet.
7. Tie yarn from the body and hands to the craft stick.
8. Move the craft stick back and forth to move the puppet.

More to Do

1. Glue a button to the back of each foot to add weight.
2. Glue "wiggly" eyes and yarn hair onto the puppet head.
3. Connect the hands and feet to the center heart with strips of construction paper folded in an "accordion fold."
4. Omit the yarn connecting the hands to the craft stick.

The Lesson Connection

The Good Samaritan: Luke 10:30–37

Read Jesus' parable of the Good Samaritan. Have the children use their puppets to show how God's children can share Jesus' love with one another. Ask children to tell how they have been Good Samaritans to others. As they tell their stories, remind them that we can show love to others because Jesus loved us first.

Plaque

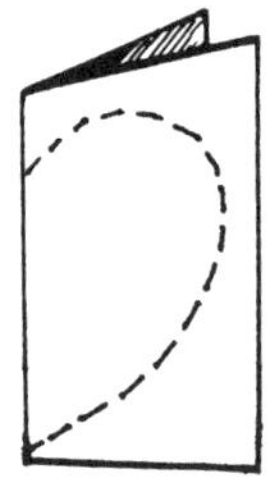

What You Need

Construction paper
Markers or crayons
Scissors
Pencil
Hole punch
Yarn or ribbon

What You Do

1. Use as a pattern the largest heart found on page 17 to trace and cut a heart. Or fold a piece of paper and cut your own heart shape along the fold (see diagram).
2. Write an appropriate message on the heart.
3. Decorate the heart by gluing on or drawing other shapes and designs.
4. Punch a hole at the top of the heart, tie a piece of yarn or ribbon through it, and hang in the classroom.

More to Do

1. Glue on sequins or other decorative trim. Write with glitter pens or glitter glue.
2. Use the heart to illustrate Bible passages telling of God's love for us.
3. Decorate the heart with heart stamps.
4. Punch holes around the heart, cut a piece of yarn, tape one end to the back, and "sew" around the outside of the heart.

The Lesson Connection

God So Loved the World: John 3:16

Have each child make a heart plaque as a reminder that God loved the world so much He sent Jesus to die on the cross for the sins of each and every person. Draw a cross on the heart. As an option, add the words, "God Loves _________ (name of child)." Have the children take their heart plaques home as a way to share the Gospel message with their families and friends.

Flowers in a Pot

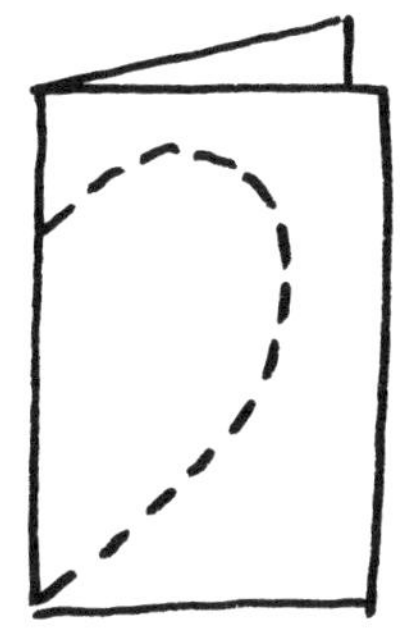

What You Need

Construction paper
Styrofoam cup
Craft sticks
Permanent marker
Scissors
Pencil
Glue

What You Do

1. Trace and cut heart shapes from construction paper (see page 17 for patterns). Or fold pieces of paper and cut hearts along the fold (see diagram).
2. Glue hearts to the end of craft sticks. Glue a single heart or several hearts together for petals.
3. With the permanent marker, write an appropriate Bible passage on the Styrofoam cup.
4. Glue additional hearts around the outside of the cup.
5. Place the flowers inside the cup.

More to Do

1. Tape the hearts to drinking straws or glue them to chenille sticks.
2. Cut hearts from craft foam and glue them to the craft sticks or chenille sticks.
3. Cut hearts and stems from poster board, construction paper, wallpaper, felt, or other materials. Glue them onto a sheet of construction paper to make a poster.
4. Make a greeting card using heart flowers.
5. Glue hearts in a circle to make a single blossom. Stick a gummed circle or glue a metallic sequin to the center.
6. Turn the cup upside down, write a Bible passage on the cup, and stick the craft sticks through the bottom.

The Lesson Connection

Grow in God's Love: 2 Thessalonians 1:3

As children make flowers, talk about how God helps us "grow" in His love as we show love to others. Write "Grow in God's Love" on each cup. Group the flowers together and count them. Write the total number of heart flowers the class made at the top of a large sheet of paper. Then, asking children for suggestions, make a list of ways to be a servant and show God's love by helping others. See if you can match the number of flowers, or maybe even come up with more!

Gift Bag

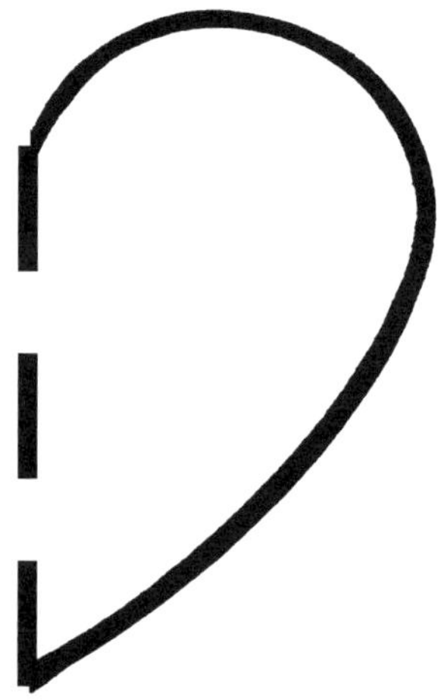

What You Need

Lunch bag
Construction paper
Pencil
Scissors
Glue
Marker or crayon
Gift
Colored tissue paper

What You Do

1. Use the heart patterns on page 17, or fold pieces of paper and cut hearts along the fold (see diagram).
2. With a marker or crayon, write an appropriate Bible verse or Christian saying on one of the hearts.
3. Glue the hearts on the bag.
4. Place colored tissue paper and a gift into the bag to give to someone else.

More to Do

1. Use a variety of colored of bags (available at craft and discount stores).
2. Use heart patterns cut from stiff paper. Trace heart outlines onto bags.
3. Decorate with heart stickers.
4. Tape heart shapes to craft sticks, straws, or chenille sticks. Place them inside a small, decorated bag.
5. Punch holes on opposite sides of the bag, and tie a yarn handle through them.

The Lesson Connection

Dorcas Shows Love: Acts 9:36–42

Read the story of Dorcas and how she showed God's love by providing clothes and food for those who needed them. As a follow-up activity, invite the children to bring school supplies that can be given to children less fortunate. Have each child sign his or her name on the outside of the bag and write "Jesus Loves You and So Do I." Fill the bags with supplies and deliver to an area mission. As you do so, thank God for the many blessings in your own lives, especially the blessing of Jesus.

Triangle Patterns

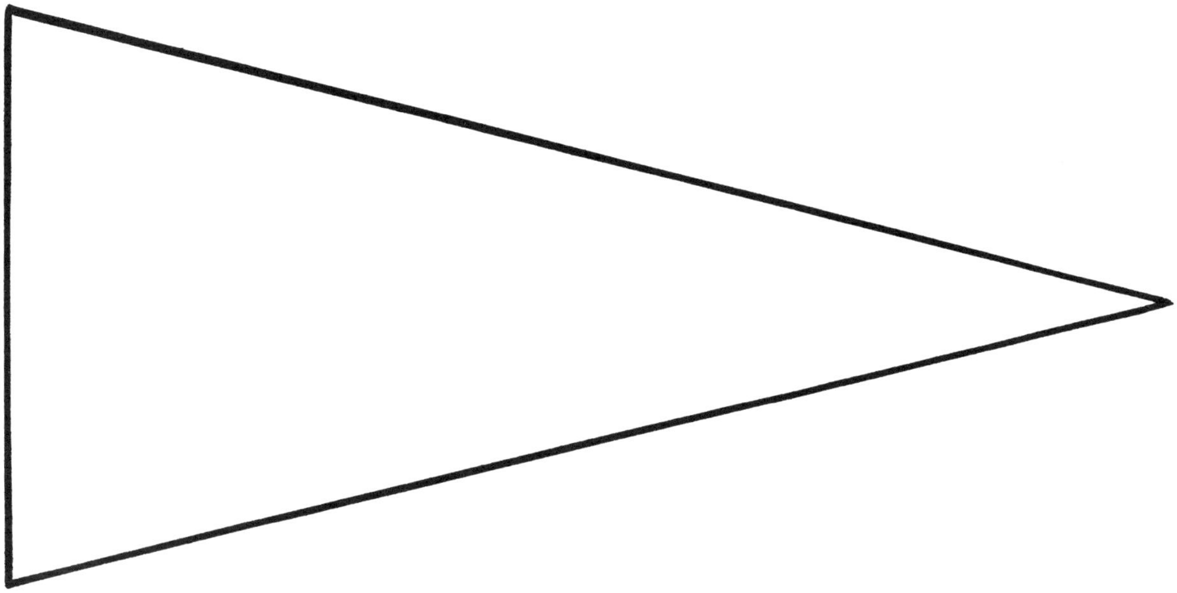

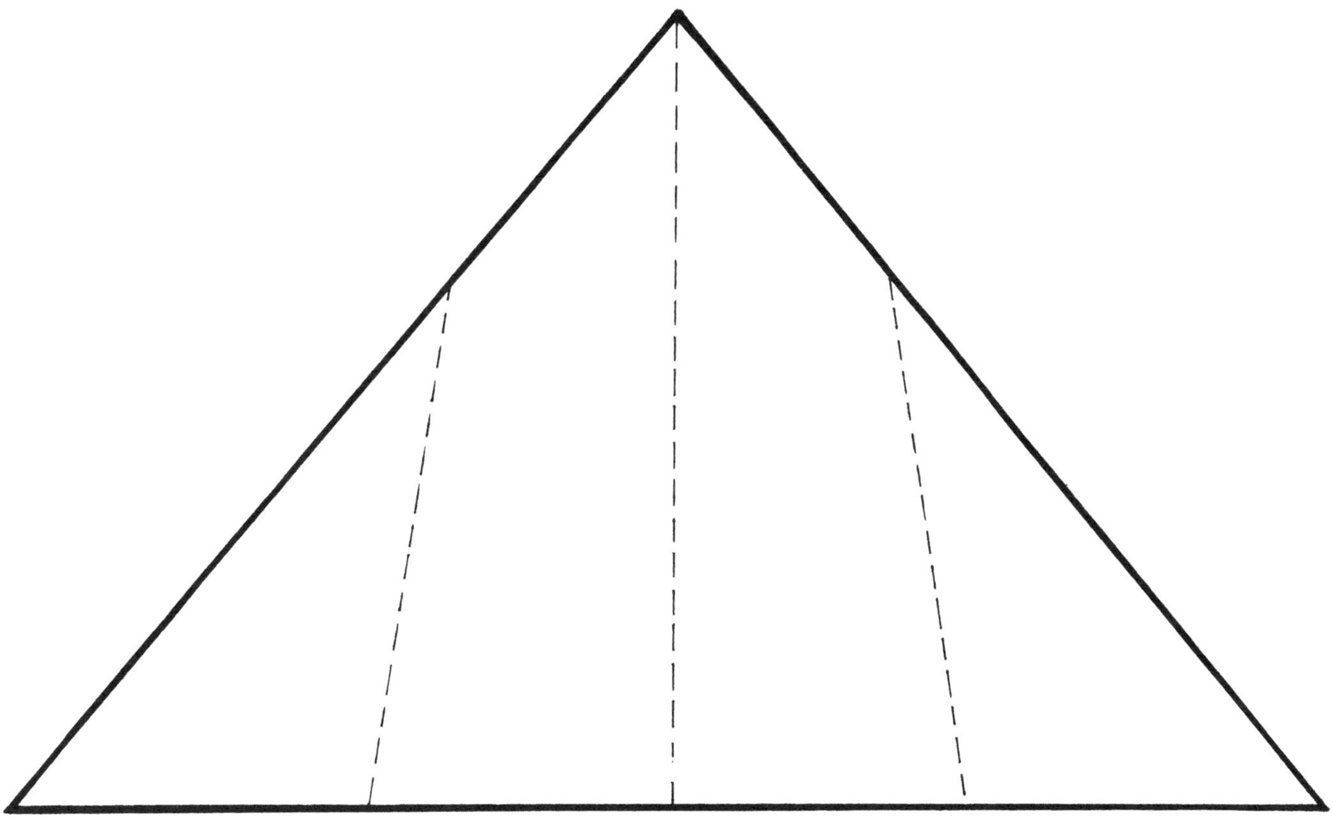

Church

More to Do

1. If your church building is triangular in shape, omit folding in the two sides of the triangle. Instead, glue a paper loop to the back to stand it up.
2. Draw the outside of the church, cut small slits to form a "T" in the bottom of the triangle, then fold back paper on each side of the "T" to make open doors (see diagram).

What You Need

Construction paper
Scissors
Markers or crayons
Pencil

What You Do

1. Trace and cut the large triangle found on page 23.
2. Ask the children to draw the inside of the church on the triangle.
3. Fold back two corners to stand up the church.

The Lesson Connection

Jesus in the Temple: Luke 2:41–50

Tell how Jesus went to His temple when He was 12 and how we also go to church, where God comes to us through His Word, through Baptism, and through the Lord's Supper. Explain how we return our thanks and praise to God through the songs we sing and the prayers we pray. We call that worship. Ask the children to draw a picture of themselves and their family worshiping God in church. As an option, sing favorite worship songs as you work.

Pennant

What You Need

Construction paper
Pencil
Scissors
Glue
Markers (optional)

What You Do

1. Use the long triangle on page 23 as a pattern.
2. Cut shapes or letters to fit on the pennant and glue them in place.
3. Trace and cut a strip of paper the length of the short side of the triangle. Cut fringe along one side of the strip and glue the opposite side to the triangle.

More to Do

1. Instead of cutting letters, draw them with markers, crayons, glitter glue, or craft paint.
2. Make pennant from felt or craft foam. Attach shapes or letters with craft glue.
3. Add glitter, sequins, or other decorative trim to the pennant.
4. Enlarge the pattern to fit your needs.

The Lesson Connection

Children Sing to Jesus: Matthew 21:14–16

The children in Jesus' time sang their praises to Him. You can make a pennant to witness your love for Him too. Draw and cut out letters to make the word "Jesus" and glue them onto the pennant banner. (If desired, use the letters shown on this page.) Hang the banners around the classroom or on a bulletin board with the heading "Hosanna! Jesus is Lord!"

Christmas Tree

What You Need

Green construction paper
Pencil
Crayons
Scissors
Gummed stars
Fine-tip marker

What You Do

1. Use as a pattern the long triangle on page 23.
2. Cut a construction paper triangle and fold it in half lengthwise to make a crease from top to bottom.
3. Use a crayon to write an appropriate Christmas word or phrase on the tree.
4. Glue a large star at the top of the tree; glue smaller stars in random places onto the tree.
5. Stand tree.

More to Do

1. Cut tree from stiff craft paper.
2. Glue on glitter yarn as garland.
3. Instead of gummed stars, add metallic craft stars, religious Christmas stickers, or colored gummed circles.
4. Decorate the tree with glitter glue, decorative trim, or shapes cut from construction paper, wrapping paper, or foil paper.
5. Use the triangle shape to make a Christmas card.

The Lesson Connection

Christmas: Luke 2:1–20

Talk about the many things we do to get ready for Christmas. Explain that making a Christmas tree Advent calendar is one way to get ready for the coming of Jesus. Write "Jesus Is Coming" on the tree. Give children gummed stars to attach to their tree for each day until Christmas. Add a star at the top on Christmas Day. Explain that our best Christmas present ever was Jesus, who came from heaven to be our Savior from sin.

Dove

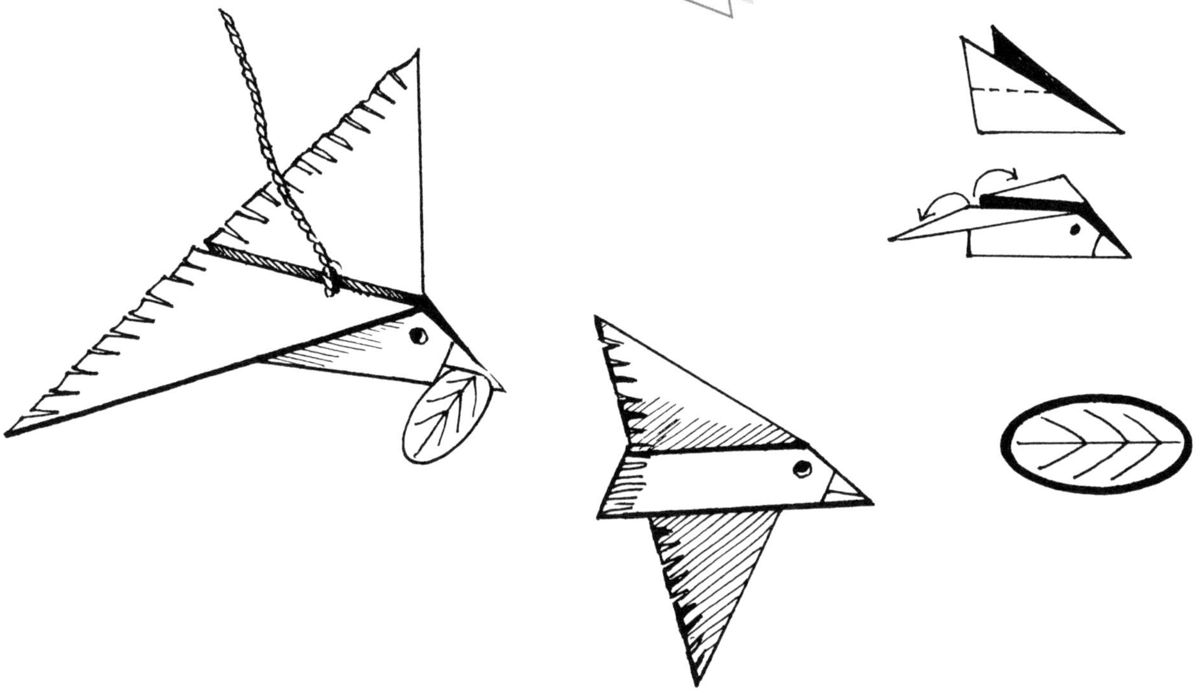

What You Need

White paper
Pencil
Markers
Scissors
Yarn

What You Do

1. Use as a pattern the triangle shapes on page 23.
2. Trace and cut a triangle from white paper.
3. Fold the triangle in half lengthwise, then fold back the corners to form wings, as shown in the diagram.
4. Use a marker to add an eye and a beak to each side of the dove.
5. Glue the center of the dove together. Glue or tape a piece of yarn to the top for hanging.
6. Cut short slits in the end to form tail feathers.
7. Hang the doves in your classroom.

More to Do

1. Make white doves to represent the Holy Spirit at the Baptism of Jesus.
2. Make birds from several colors of paper and hang them from a coat hanger. Use the birds to teach children about the many kinds of birds God has made.

The Lesson Connection

Noah Sends out a Dove: Genesis 8:6–11

Have each child make a white dove. Then have each child cut a green oval and fringe it to represent a leaf; cut a slit in the dove's beak, slip in the leaf, and glue it in place. Use this activity to discuss how God keeps His promises. Noah sent a dove out from the ark and it brought back an olive branch. God kept His promise to keep Noah and his family safe and dry. And God kept the greatest promise of all: He sent His Son to be our Savior.

Star Puppet

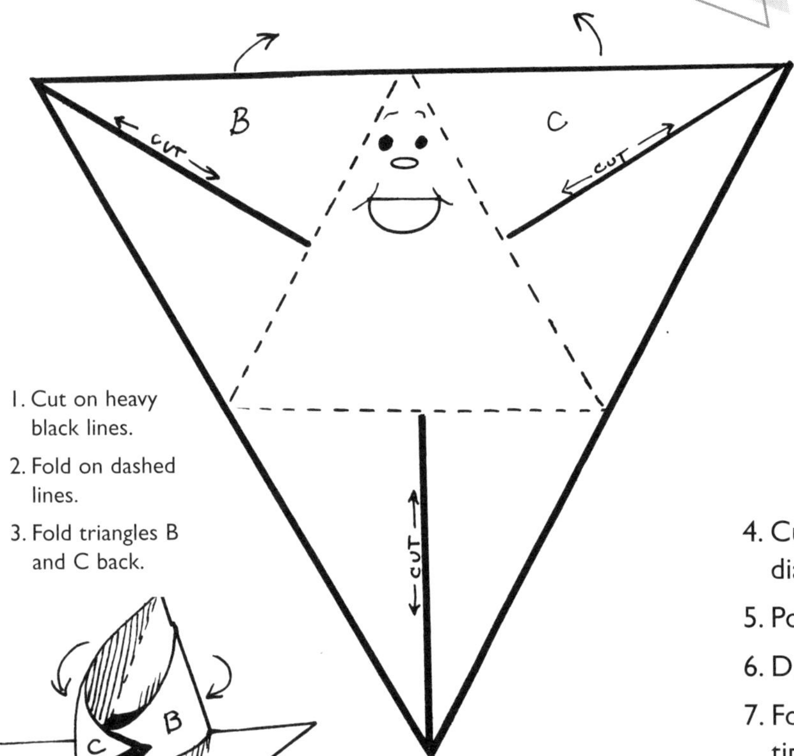

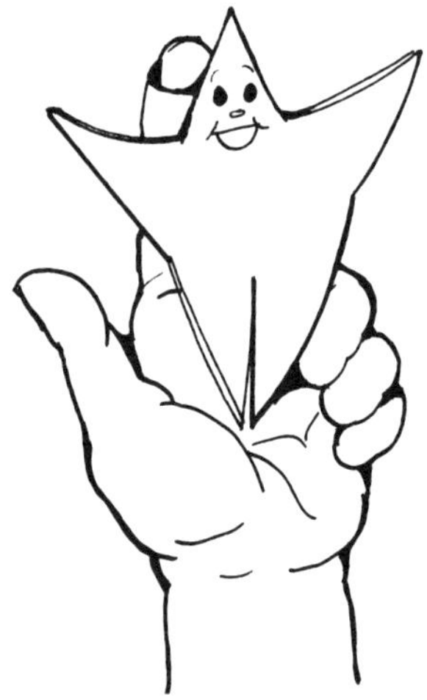

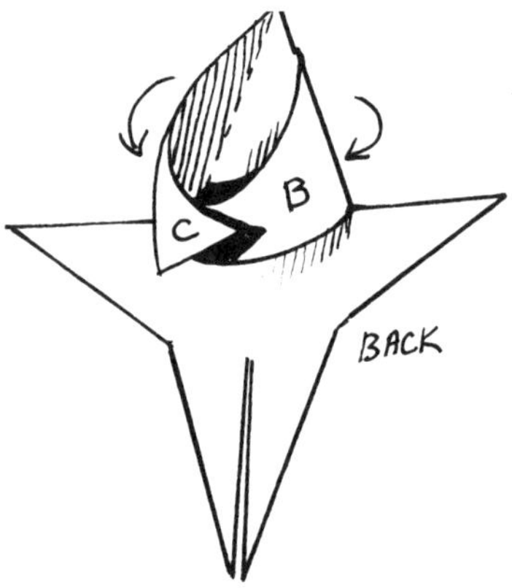

What You Need

Yellow construction paper
Pencil
Scissors
Marker
Glue

What You Do

1. Use as a pattern the triangle at the top of this page.
2. Trace and cut a triangle from yellow paper.
3. Fold in each point of the triangle to meet the opposite side (see diagram).
4. Cut a slit along the folds from each point (see diagram).
5. Position the triangle with point A at the top.
6. Draw a happy face in the top third of the star.
7. Fold points B and C to the back and glue the tips of the points to fit your finger.

More to Do

1. Glue on movable eyes or draw eyes with a glitter pen.
2. Glue foil wrapping paper to lightweight poster board, then cut out a star puppet.
3. Let each child make a star puppet to represent him- or herself shining like a star as he or she shows Jesus' love to others (Philippians 2:15).

The Lesson Connection

Wise Men: Matthew 2:1–11

Have each child make a star puppet to represent the star that led the Wise Men to the Christ Child. Explain that just as the Wise Men came to Bethlehem to worship Jesus, we can go to church to worship Jesus, our Savior and King. Encourage the children to take their star puppets home and use them to invite a special someone to church and Sunday School.

Star Patterns

Mobile

What You Need

Construction paper
Pencil
Scissors
Yarn
Hole punch
Coat hanger

What You Do

1. Use as patterns the stars here or on page 29.
2. Cut as many stars as desired.
3. Punch a hole at the top of each star and tie a piece of yarn through it.
4. Tie each star to the bottom of the coat hanger. Hang the coat hanger in your classroom.

More to Do

1. Decorate stars with glitter glue or glitter paint.
2. Use the stars to make a classroom bulletin board with a picture of Abraham looking at the star-filled sky. Add the words "God Keeps His Promises" to the board.
3. Trace stars onto foil wrapping. Cut two stars, glue one end of yarn to the back of one star, then glue on second star with shiny side out.

The Lesson Connection

God Created the Heavens: Genesis 1:14–17

Make the star mobile to teach children that God created the many heavenly bodies set in the sky. (If desired, add other objects God placed in the sky, such as planets and moons.) Make a large star to hang from the middle of the mobile with the words "God Made the Stars." As children work, tell them that stars can remind us that God is all-powerful. Explain that since God made the stars and keeps them in the sky, we can know that He is Lord over all and that He will continue to care for His entire creation, us included.

Crown

What You Need

Construction paper
Pencil
Scissors
Glue

What You Do

1. Copy and trace a star pattern on this page or on page 29. Cut enough stars to go around a child's head.
2. Glue the stars together in ring to make a crown.

More to Do

1. Tape the stars together.
2. Make stars from several colors of construction paper, poster board, or wrapping paper.
3. Add lettering and details to stars with glitter glue, crayons, or fabric paint.

The Lesson Connection

God's Children "Shine Like Stars": Philippians 2:15

Write each letter for "JESUS" onto five stars and glue them together. Add enough additional stars to make a crown that fits around each child's head. As they work, talk about ways the children can be "shining stars," shining the love of Jesus by what they say and do. Remind them that God has made them His own and that He will help them shine His love to others.

Star Stick

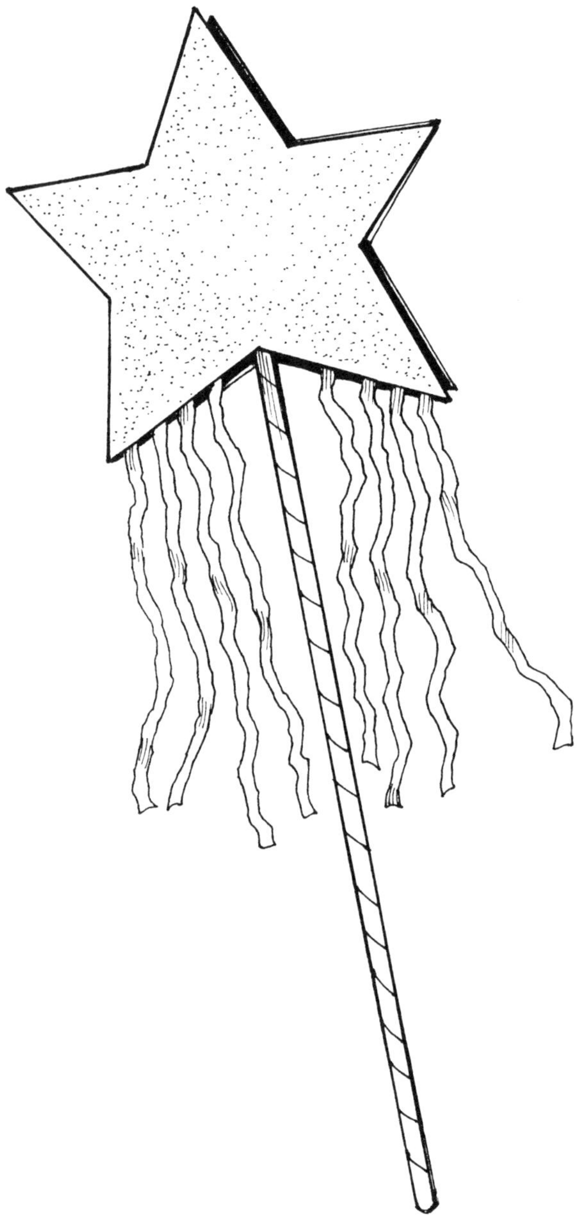

What You Do

1. Use a star pattern on page 29 to cut two construction paper stars.
2. Glue thin foil strips along the bottom of one of the stars.
3. Glue the end of the drinking straw onto the back of that star. Match the other star, and with wrong sides facing, glue the two stars together.
4. If desired, decorate the front of the star with glitter glue.

More to Do

1. Color with glitter crayons instead of glitter glue.
2. Cover the star with glue and sprinkle on glitter.
3. Use a wooden dowel or craft stick instead of a drinking straw.
4. Cut stars from foil paper, wrapping paper, or poster board.
5. Substitute metallic ribbon or tinsel for thin foil strips.

What You Need

Yellow construction paper
Drinking straw
Thin foil strips
Craft glue
Glitter glue
Scissors
Pencil

The Lesson Connection

Epiphany: Matthew 2:1–11

Make a star to use as a visual aid while you tell the story of the Magi. Take turns having children hold the star and lead the others around the room in a game of "Follow the Star." Sing a hymn such as "We Three Kings," "O Morning Star, How Fair and Bright," "As with Gladness Men of Old," or "Brightest and Best of the Stars of the Morning." Add that God leads us to Jesus through His Word, the Bible, and through our pastors, teachers, and parents.

Yarn Star Ornament

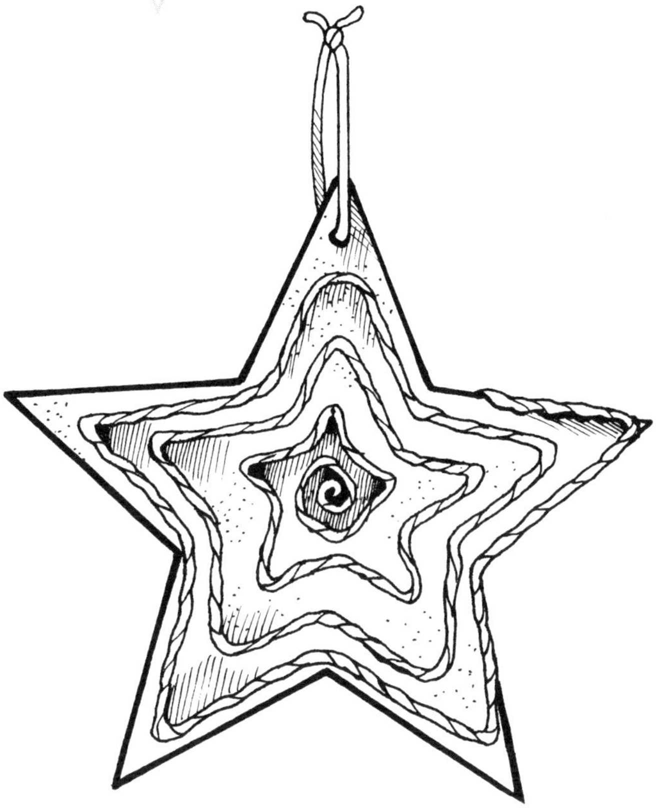

More to Do

1. Use glitter yarn.
2. Glue yarn onto felt stars.
3. Use other shapes in this book to make yarn ornaments.
4. Use this activity with the story of the Wise Men. Explain that this Mexican folk art technique reminds us that Jesus came for people everywhere.

What You Need

Poster board or heavy paper
Yarn
Pencil
Scissors
Hole punch
Glue

What You Do

1. Use the star here or one on page 29 to copy and cut a star from poster board or heavy paper.
2. Cut a piece of yarn and glue it over the star, either in a random design or in concentric circles, until the star shape is filled in completely.
3. Glue a piece of yarn to the back of the star as a hanger, or punch a hole at the top of the star, thread yarn through the hole, and tie.

The Lesson Connection

Jesus, Star of Jacob: Numbers 24:17a

Jesus was once called the "Star of Jacob." Make star ornaments for the classroom Christmas tree to help the children remember this name. As they work, tell them about other names the Bible gives us for Jesus. Explain that the names given to Jesus told Old Testament people how He would fulfill God's promise to send a Savior. Now that we know how Jesus died and rose again, we can tell others too.

Tissue-Paper Sun Catcher

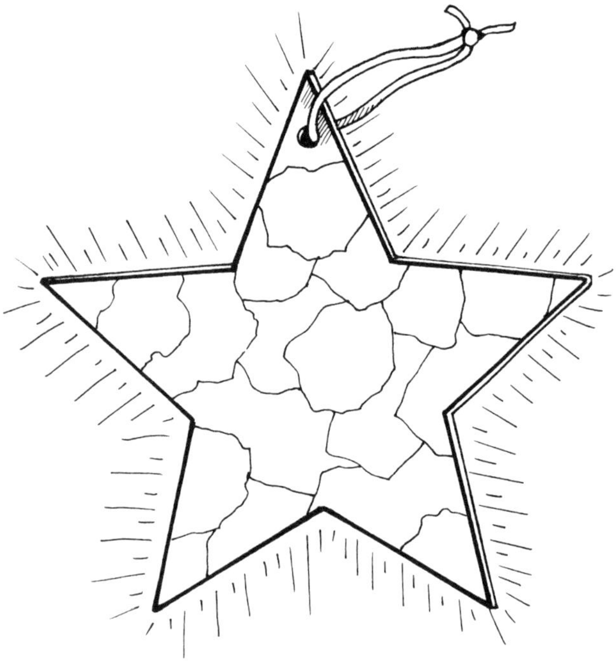

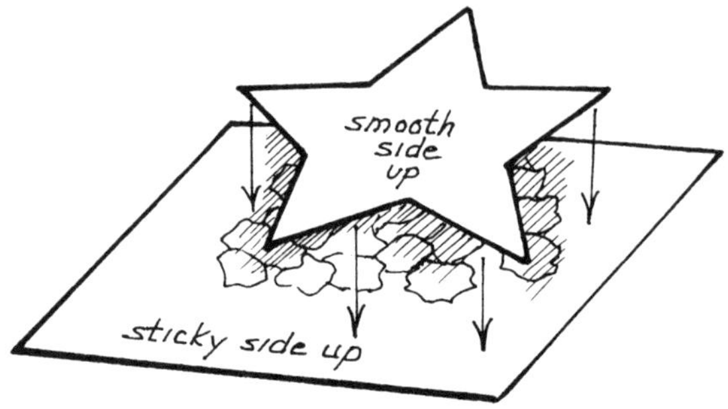

6. Trace and cut a star from the vinyl.
7. Punch a hole at the top of the star and tie a piece of yarn through the hole for hanging.

What You Need

Clear self-adhesive vinyl
Yellow tissue paper (additional colors optional)
Pencil
Scissors
Hole punch
Yarn

What You Do

1. Use as a pattern a star on page 29.
2. Cut or tear tissue paper into small pieces.
3. From the clear vinyl, cut two squares or circles slightly bigger than the star pattern you've chosen.
4. Pull off the backing of one of the vinyl shapes. Place small, tissue-paper pieces onto the sticky side to overlap at random until the shape is completely covered.
5. Remove the backing of the second shape and match it to the tissue-paper side of the first shape. You will have vinyl on each side and tissue paper in the middle.

More to Do

1. Omit the second piece of vinyl so there is just one vinyl star.
2. On the tissue-paper side, before adding the second piece of vinyl, use a permanent marker to draw in "stained-glass window lines" over the star. Or add a short caption or Bible verse to the front of the star.
3. Instead of a star, use another shape found in this book.

The Lesson Connection

God Created the Sun and the Stars: Genesis 1:14–17

Have each child make a star to hang in the classroom window. As you work, talk about how God uses the sun, our closest star, to bless our world. Compare how we need the sun to replace the darkness to how Jesus came to take the darkness of sin away. Talk about how plants need the sun to grow and how we need Jesus to help us grow.

Square Patterns

Stand-Up Plaque

What You Need

Sturdy or stiff white paper
Sticker
Marker
Pencil
Scissors

What You Do

1. Use as a pattern a large square on page 35.
2. Trace and cut a square, then fold it in half.
3. On the bottom half of the folded square, place a sticker and write an appropriate Bible passage or religious saying.
4. Stand up the folded square.

More to Do

1. Use any verse from the Bible or have children write their own words or saying.
2. Instead of a sticker, glue on a shape found in this book.
3. Instead of a sticker, have children draw a small picture relating to the Bible verse they've chosen.
4. Substitute a rectangle for a square.
5. Use stand-up plaques as place cards at a special lunch or banquet.

The Lesson Connection

David Sings to God: Psalm 98

Read Psalm 98. Write several short phrases or verses from this psalm or another one on the board. Have each child pick a phrase or verse to write on his or her square. If the children are old enough, have them copy a phrase or verse onto their square. If not, have them tell you which one they want you to write on their square. As you work together, talk about the many ways we give our praise to God in thanks for all He has done for us.

Dogwood Flower

What You Need

White construction paper
Yellow circle sticker
Pencil
Ruler
Red crayon
Scissors
Chenille stick
Tape

What You Do

1. Use as a pattern a square on page 35.
2. Cut a white square.
3. Fold the square along the diagonal to form a triangle. Unfold it, then fold a second time along the opposite diagonal to form a triangle. Unfold it. There will be two creases that look like an X.
4. Attach the yellow circle sticker to the center of the square.
5. Cut along the fold line from each point to the edge of the circle to make four flower petals.
6. Draw a small red spot in the middle of the outside edge of each petal.
7. Use a pencil to slightly curl in the side of each petal.
8. Tape the back of the flower to the pipe cleaner.

More to Do

1. Instead of a dogwood blossom, use different colored paper to make other kinds of flowers.
2. Substitute a cut circle, heart, or triangle for the flower center.
3. Stick the end of the pipe cleaner through the center of the flower, then glue the circle over it.

The Lesson Connection

Jesus Died on the Cross for Our Sins: Matthew 27:45–54

Dogwoods bloom in early spring, the same time of year we observe Lent. Explain how the blossom can help us remember that Jesus died on the cross for us. It has four petals just like a cross has four parts. The spots of red at the end of each petal remind us of the wounds in His hands and feet. Make a Lenten bouquet. Then have each child write a prayer to Jesus, thanking Him for springtime and New Life in Him.

Candle

What You Need

Construction paper
Yellow tissue paper
Fine-tip marker
Glue
Pencil
Scissors

What You Do

1. Use as a pattern the square on this page.
2. Cut yellow tissue paper into squares.
3. Cut a construction paper square. Draw a cross on the square.
4. Roll the square into a tube and glue or tape the edges.
5. Place the eraser end of a pencil in the center of the tissue square, gather the tissue around the pencil, then glue the end inside the paper tube to make the candle flame.

More to Do

1. Make four candles, one for each of the four weeks before Christmas, and place them around a wreath base cut from a circle or paper plate. Cut small green tissue paper squares, twist them around the eraser end of a pencil, and glue them to the wreath.
2. Use metallic paper or colored cellophane for the candle flame and decorative paper for the candle. Glue on a ribbon or construction paper cross.

The Lesson Connection

The Lord Is My Light: Psalm 27:1

Consider using two pieces of ribbon to make the cross on the candle before gluing the candle together. Sing "This Little Gospel Light of Mine" as you work. Explain to the children what Jesus meant when He called Himself the Light of the world. Share how the Good News of Jesus and His love is for everyone.

Picture Frame

What You Need

Sturdy or stiff paper
Fine-tip markers
Photograph
Hole punch
Yarn
Tape
Scissors
Pencil

What You Do

1. Use as patterns a large square and a medium square on page 35.
2. Cut two large paper squares.
3. With the medium square as a pattern, cut a hole in the center of one of the large squares that is large enough for the photograph to show through but smaller than the photo itself.
4. Hold the two squares together and punch around three sides with a hole punch.
5. Cut a piece of yarn; knot one end and tape the other. With the taped end of the yarn, lace around the three sides of the square. Knot and tape the yarn to the back when finished.
6. Use markers to write a phrase or draw pictures on the frame.
7. Slip the picture inside the frame.

More to Do

1. Omit lacing and glue three sides of the frame together.
2. Glue or trace onto the frame other shapes found in this book.
3. Write on the frame with glitter glue or fabric paint. Glue on sequins or decorative fabric trim.
4. Make the frame from craft foam sheets.

The Lesson Connection

God Created People: Genesis 1:7, 1:18–24

Have the children place photographs of themselves inside their frames to celebrate that they are unique and special creations of God. Write "I am God's Child" on the frame. Remind the children that although God made each of us different, there is something the same about each of us: We all need Jesus as our Savior.

Cross

What You Need

Construction paper
Pencil
Scissors
Glue

What You Do

1. Use as patterns the large square and a small square on page 35.
2. Trace and cut one large construction paper square.
3. Trace and cut five small squares of a second color.
4. On the large square, arrange the five small squares to form a cross. Glue small squares in place (see illustration).

More to Do

1. Add a third row of very small squares. Glue on one small square for each of the six weeks in Lent. Add a flower sticker to the center square on Easter Day.
2. Make a Joy cross: write the word "JOY" across and down the squares so the Os intersect at the center.

The Lesson Connection

Jesus Died and Rose Again: Mark 15:33–37, 16:2–7

Use this activity as an opportunity to discuss both the sad and happy feelings of Good Friday and Easter. Glue five purple squares to a larger black square. In the center square write "He died for me." Discuss the sadness we feel because Jesus had to die for us. Then cut and glue very bright-colored squares on the other side to form another cross. In the center square write "He lives for me." Discuss the joy we feel because He rose again. Punch a hole at the top and attach a yarn loop for hanging. Review the Easter story and tell the children that after He rose from the grave, Jesus told His followers to spread the Good News of His love to the whole world. We call this the Great Commission and, as His followers, we are part of this Great Commission too!

Rectangle Patterns

Tube Puppet

What You Need

Construction paper
Markers or crayons
Scissors
Glue
Pencil

What You Do

1. Use as a pattern the large rectangle on page 41 or the one shown here. Trace and cut a rectangle from construction paper.
2. Place the long side of the rectangle in front of you and draw a figure in the center of it.
3. Glue the short sides of the rectangle to form a tube and stand it up.

More to Do

1. Cut figures from old Sunday School lesson leaflets and glue onto the rectangle.
2. Use small tube puppets as finger puppets.
3. Glue or tape craft sticks or plastic drinking straws inside the bottom of tube puppets to turn them into stick puppets.
4. Instead of gluing the tube together, tape it.

The Lesson Connection

The Parable of the Lost Sheep: Matthew 18:12–14

Use the patterns on this page to cut two rectangles. Draw a shepherd on the larger rectangle and a sheep on the other. Glue short sides together to make the puppets. Use them to tell the parable of how a shepherd with 100 sheep lost one. He left the 99 and searched until he found his lost sheep. Discuss how Jesus is our Good Shepherd, always caring for and protecting us. Sing "I Am Jesus' Little Lamb." Ask for volunteers to pray aloud, thanking the Good Shepherd for His love and care.

Storytelling Tube

What You Need

Construction paper
Markers or crayons
Glue
Scissors
Pencil

What You Do

1. Use as a pattern the rectangle on page 41 or cut your own rectangle.
2. Choose a Bible story that has at least two or three scenes.
3. Place the rectangle lengthwise in front of you.
4. Draw the scenes of the story in sequence on the rectangle.
5. Glue the edges of the tube together and stand it up.
6. Turn the tube as you tell the story.

More to Do

1. Use poster board to make a large storytelling tube.
2. Have different students draw each part of the story.
3. Instead of drawing figures, cut them from old Sunday School lesson leaflets.
4. Use simple outlines and stick figures for smaller tubes.

The Lesson Connection

The Ten Commandments: Deuteronomy 5:6–22

Use the tube to tell the story of the Ten Commandments. Draw Mt. Sinai in the center of the rectangle. Add Moses standing on the mountain. On the left side, draw Moses walking toward the mountain. On the right side, draw Moses walking away from the mountain, carrying the stone tablets. Glue the short sides of the rectangle together and turn the tube as you tell the story. Review the Ten Commandments. Explain that no one can keep God's commandments perfectly, although we try really hard. Then explain that God knows we aren't perfect and that's why He sent Jesus. He lived a perfect life and kept all the commandments for us. Then He died on the cross so we can be forgiven for every sin. We can ask God to help us keep the commandments and thank Him for His forgiveness.

Napkin Ring

What You Need

Construction paper
Markers or crayons
Napkins
Glue
Scissors
Pencil

What You Do

1. Trace a rectangle from page 41. Cut from construction paper.
2. Write an appropriate Bible verse or phrase onto the rectangle. Add appropriate decorations.
3. Glue the short ends of the rectangle to form a ring.
4. Roll up a napkin and place it inside the napkin ring.

More to Do

1. Make the napkin ring from fabric, felt, or wrapping paper.
2. Use a computer to type and print prayers, then glue prayers onto the napkin ring.
3. Write Bible passages on the rectangle, then glue the ends to make the napkin ring.
4. Add decorative stickers to the napkin ring.

The Lesson Connection

God Sends Manna: Exodus 16:3–18

Write "Thank God for His Goodness" on the rectangle before gluing it into a napkin ring. Tell the Bible story, then have each child make enough napkin rings for each member of his or her family. Tell them to take the napkin rings home and tell their family the Bible story. The napkin rings can help us remember that God provides for us and feeds us, just like He provided for His children in the wilderness

Place Mat

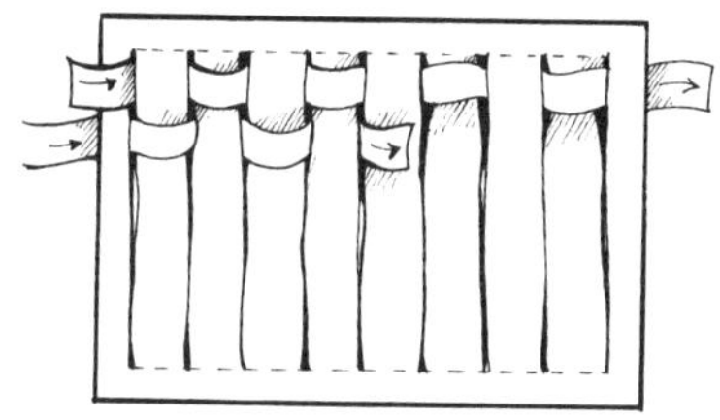

What You Need

Construction paper
Ruler
Pencil
Scissors
Glue

What You Do

1. Use a full sheet of construction paper for your rectangle.
2. With a ruler as a guide, lightly draw a frame about 1" inside each side of the rectangle.
3. Trace parallel lines about 1" apart along the width of the rectangle. Cut along lines, being careful to cut only to the frame.
4. Cut strips of paper the length of the rectangle.
5. Start at one end of the rectangle and weave a strip of paper over-and-under the cut lines.
6. Glue down the ends of the strip.
7. Repeat with a second strip, weaving under-and-over instead of over-and-under. Alternate the weaving of the strips until the place mat is filled in.
8. Write a Bible verse or phrase onto the place mat.

More to Do

1. Use clear self-adhesive vinyl to cover the place mat.
2. Laminate the place mat.
3. Instead of straight lines, cut wavy lines along the width of the place mat.
4. Glue a second rectangle with a prayer or Bible verse to the center of the place mat.
5. Cut weaving strips from a different color.
6. Use your weaving for a poster, not a place mat.
7. Glue on a paper circle for a plate, and cut paper food. Glue to the place mat.

The Lesson Connection

The Ten Lepers: Luke 17:11–19

Trace your hand, fingers together, onto a piece of construction paper. Cut out the hand. Write or draw things for which you are thankful onto the hand. As children work, tell the Bible story. Then ask the children what they can thank Jesus for. As they finish the project, explain that we can be most thankful for Jesus, who brings us salvation and eternal life.

Wind Sock

What You Do

1. Use the rectangles on page 41 as patterns. Or make large rectangle patterns of your own.
2. Trace and cut out the large rectangle. Write words or draw appropriate shapes on it, or cut and glue on letters or shapes.
3. Cut narrow construction paper strips and glue them along the bottom of the large rectangle on the inside of one of the long sides.
4. Glue the short sides of the large rectangle together to make a tube.
5. Punch two holes in opposite sides at the top of the tube.
6. Cut a piece of yarn and tie ends in each hole. Hang the wind sock in your classroom.

More to Do

1. Substitute ribbon or crepe paper for strips of construction paper.
2. Glue decorative fabric trim or sequins to the wind sock.
2. Hang metal spoons from a cardboard rectangle to make "wind chimes."

What You Need

Construction paper
Pencil
Markers
Ruler
Glue
Hole punch
Yarn
Scissors

The Lesson Connection

Jesus Enters Jerusalem: Mark 11:1–10

Use bright, happy colors to make a Palm Sunday wind sock. Write "Hosanna" and draw palm branches on the rectangle before gluing the sides together. Discuss how happy we feel because Jesus, the Promised One, came to save us. Memorize Mark 11:9: "Hosanna! Blessed is He who comes in the name of the Lord!" Chant the verse as you walk around your church or school, waving your wind socks behind you, leading a palm parade.

Wreath

Shapes used: circle, rectangle, triangle, and oval

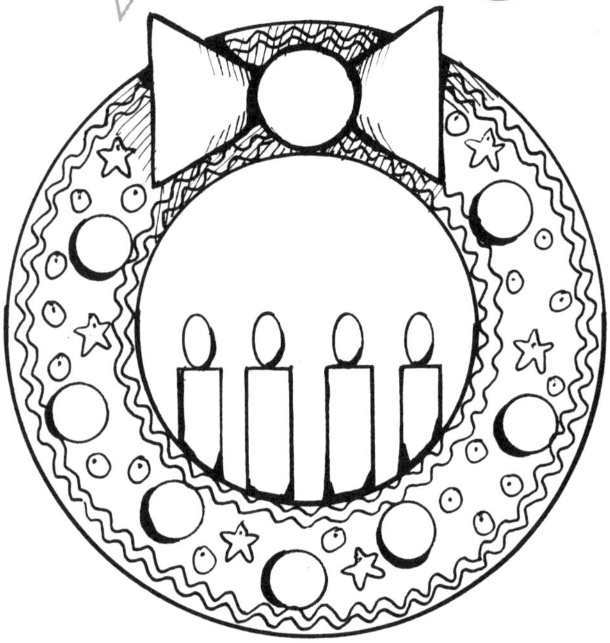

What You Need

Construction paper (green, red, and yellow)
Pencil
Scissors
Hole punch (optional)

What You Do

1. Use the large and medium circle patterns on page 5. Use the large circle as a pattern and cut the outside circle from green construction paper. Cut the medium circle from the center to make a ring. Or cut the wreath shape from a large circle found in your classroom.
2. Using the illustration on this page as a guide, cut two red triangles and one red circle to glue together for a bow.
3. Glue the bow onto the top of the wreath.
4. Cut four red rectangles and glue or tape them along the bottom of the wreath (from the inside) to make candles. Cut four yellow ovals and glue one to the top of each candle.

More to Do

1. Cut green and red tissue paper squares. Twist the center of each square around the eraser end of a pencil. Glue each tissue twist to the wreath until it is covered. Or glue on wadded tissue paper squares.
2. Cut the wreath and bow from craft foam. Add a magnet to the back or a yarn loop to the top.
3. Glue sequins, fabric trim, or colored circles to the wreath.

The Lesson Connection

Advent: Luke 1:26–56

These Bible verses tell how Mary prepared for the coming of Jesus. Advent is the time when we prepare for the coming of Jesus. Instead of the traditional way to use the Advent wreath, consider omitting the candles and adding a red circle sticker for each day during Advent (or four stickers, one for each week in Advent). Another option is to add the candles and glue one oval flame to a candle for each week in Advent. Each time you add a sticker or a flame, talk about how you can "keep Jesus in Christmas" as you get ready for His birthday.

Paper Ornament

Shapes used: circle and optional shapes

What You Need

Construction paper
Yarn
Pencil
Scissors
Hole punch
Glue

What You Do

1. Trace and cut a circle to use as a background and another shape.
2. Glue the shape to the circle.
3. Punch a hole at the top of the circle. Cut a piece of yarn, thread it through the hole, and tie it to make a hanger.

More to Do

1. Cut paper circles and shapes to fit inside plastic lids. Glue each shape to a plastic lid.
2. Use felt, craft foam sheets, or decorative wrapping paper to make ornaments.
3. Trace patterns onto paper and have children color in or cut and glue in their own ornament.

The Lesson Connection

Jesus Is Born: Luke 2:1–17

Talk about how each of the shapes used for these ornaments can remind us of Christ's birth. ***Heart:*** God loves us and sent Jesus to be our Savior. ***Cross:*** Jesus came to die on the cross for our sins. ***Star:*** Wise Men followed the star to find Jesus. Write these explanations in a short note to send home to parents so they too can understand the connection. This is a great way to share the Gospel with parents or others who might not know that Jesus came at Christmas to be our Savior.

Jesus in the Manger

Shapes used: circle, rectangle, oval, circle, and star

What You Need

Construction paper
Pencil
Scissors
Glue

What You Do

1. Use the patterns above. Cut one large and two small rectangles from brown construction paper. Glue them to a full sheet of construction paper to make a manger. See illustration.
2. Cut a long yellow strip, then cut off pieces in desired lengths and glue them above the manger for straw.
3. Cut a large half-oval for baby Jesus' body and a small half-circle for head. Glue them above the manger.
4. Cut a yellow star and glue it above Jesus in the manger. If desired, cut and glue on yellow rectangles as rays of light.

More to Do

1. Use shapes to make a craft foam ornament or felt banner.
2. Use a photocopier to enlarge the shape patterns.

The Lesson Connection

Shepherds Share the News of Jesus' Birth: Luke 2:8–20

Make a Christmas card sharing the news of the Savior's birth. Fold a sheet of construction paper in half, then glue the shapes to make a picture of Jesus in the manger. Add an appropriate message or a Bible verse inside the card. Invite each child to share his or her card with someone they know who does not go to church. Remind the children that the shepherds, who came to worship baby Jesus, told everyone they met that they had found the Savior. We can be like the shepherds and tell others about Jesus. Sing "Away in the Manger" or "Go Tell It on the Mountain."

Angel Ornament

Shapes used: triangle, circle, and half-circle

What You Need

Construction paper
Yarn
Pencil
Fine-tip marker
Scissors
Glue
Yarn

What You Do

1. Use the patterns on page 47 to cut the angel's head, body, arms, and wings.
2. Glue the wings to back of the body. Then glue the head and arms to the front of the body and wings.
3. Cut a small piece of yarn, fringe both ends, then glue it to the top of the angel's head for hair.
4. Use a fine-tip marker to draw facial details.
5. Glue a loop of yarn behind the head for a hanger.

More to Do

1. Use wallpaper, wrapping paper, felt, or craft foam instead of construction paper.
2. Use foil wrapping paper for the angel's wings or body.
3. Cut a round paper doily or paper plate in half for the angel's wings.
4. Fold a piece of paper and glue an angel to the front to make a Christmas card.

The Lesson Connection

Angels Appear to the Shepherds: Luke 2:8–20

Add letters to a hallway or bulletin board to spell the words "Glory to God." Use yarn to hang the children's angel ornaments around the message. As you work, sing "Angels We Have Heard on High." Ask the children to tell the Bible story in their own words. Encourage them to think of ways they can share the Good News with people they know.

Crayon Sun Catcher

Shapes used: circle and optional shapes

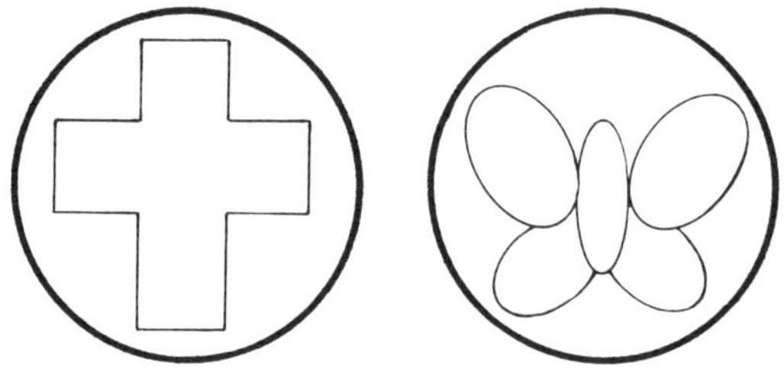

What You Need

Paper
Crayons
Cooking oil
Napkins
Styrofoam plate
Hole punch
Yarn
Pencil
Scissors

What You Do

1. Cut a paper circle. Draw a design in the center of the circle with crayons. Press firmly so all parts of the circle are completely colored.
2. Pour a small amount of cooking oil into the plate, and with the napkin rub oil over the circle. With a second napkin, rub off excess oil.
3. Let the ornament dry, then punch a hole at the top and tie a piece of yarn through it for a hanger.
4. Hang the sun catcher in a window so sunlight shines through it.

More to Do

1. Mix equal parts water and white glue. Cut or tear small pieces of colored tissue paper and dip in glue mixture. Place tissue paper on a plastic lid and let dry. Trace a shape onto black paper and cut out. Glue shape to tissue-paper side of lid. Punch a hole in the lid and string yarn through for a hanger. Hang in the classroom.
2. Use a permanent marker to trace the outline of the shape onto a plastic lid. Use white glue and water to glue on pieces of colored tissue.
3. Enlarge or reduce shapes with a photocopier.
4. Cut shapes from construction paper and outline them with glitter glue, craft paint, yarn, or decorative trim.
5. Cut the shapes from paper and glue them back-to-back. Hang shapes from dowel to make a mobile.

The Lesson Connection

Jesus Died and Rose Again: Matthew 28:1–10

Use the illustration on this page as a guide to make cross and butterfly sun catchers. Put up the cross sun catcher during Lent. Replace it with the butterfly at Easter. As you work, talk about how the two shapes remind us that Jesus died for our sins and rose again.

Palm Branch

Shapes used: oval and rectangle

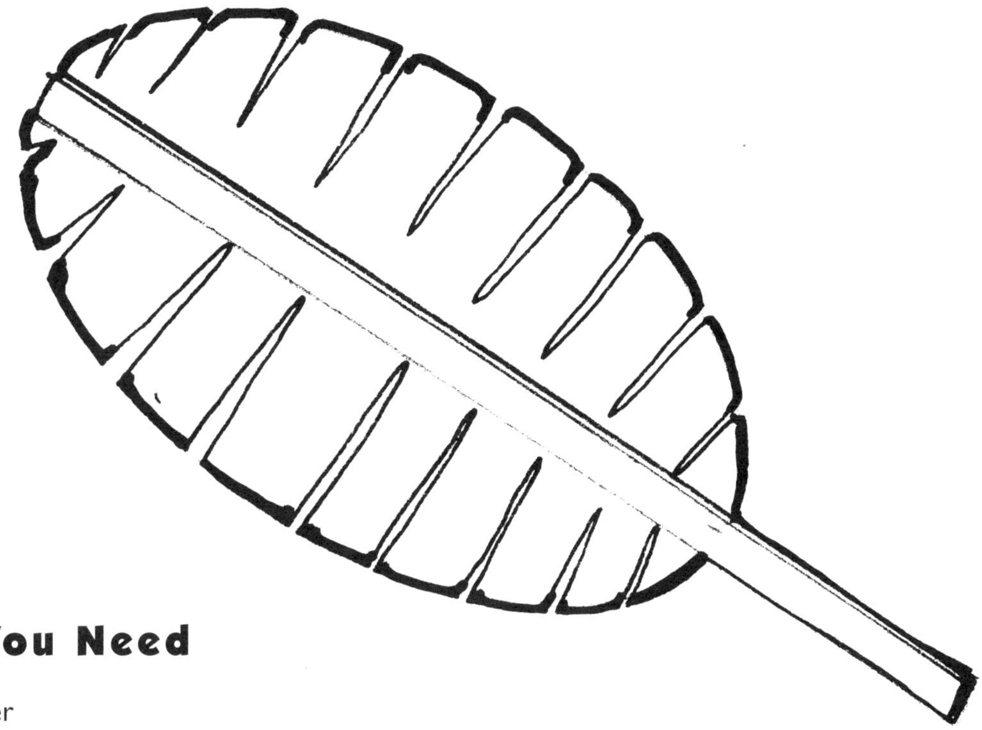

What You Need

Green construction paper
Pencil
Scissors
Glue

What You Do

1. Trace and cut a green oval and rectangle.
2. Glue the strip along the center of the oval.
3. Cut fringe around the sides of the oval.

More to Do

1. Glue a drinking straw along the center of the palm branch.
2. Use the palm branch pattern to make a felt banner. Use glitter glue or fabric paint to write the words "Hosanna" on the banner.

The Lesson Connection

Jesus Enters Jerusalem: Luke 19:29–38

Palm Sunday is the first day of Holy Week, the most significant week in the history of the world. Let each child make a palm branch to glue onto a classroom poster that has the word "Hosanna" written in the center. Or add the branches to a bulletin board with the same heading. As the children work, have them sing the following song to the melody "Jimmy, Crack Corn."

> "Hosanna," the people sang;
> "Hosanna," the people sang;
> "Hosanna," the people sang
> To Jesus Christ, their King!

Lord's Supper Picture

Shapes used: triangle, half-circle, and oval

What You Need

Construction paper (gold and brown)
Pencil
Scissors
Glue

What You Do

1. Using patterns here, cut one gold triangle, one gold half-circle, and one brown oval.
2. Glue the two parts of the cup together, then glue the bread to the bottom of the cup. See the diagram for placement.

More to Do

1. Glue the shapes onto a circle background.
2. Cut the shapes from felt and glue them onto a banner.

The Lesson Connection

The Last Supper: Matthew 26:26–28

The Lord's Supper is often a mystery to children. Take your children to the sanctuary and ask your pastor to show them the Communion ware. Ask him if it would also be okay to invite the children to touch and/or taste the Communion wafers. Ask your pastor to share the words Jesus said as He gave the bread and wine to His disciples during the Last Supper. Share that the same words are part of Holy Communion when those who receive the body and blood of Christ in the bread and wine also receive forgiveness of sins.

Stained-Glass Window

Shapes used: half circle and rectangle

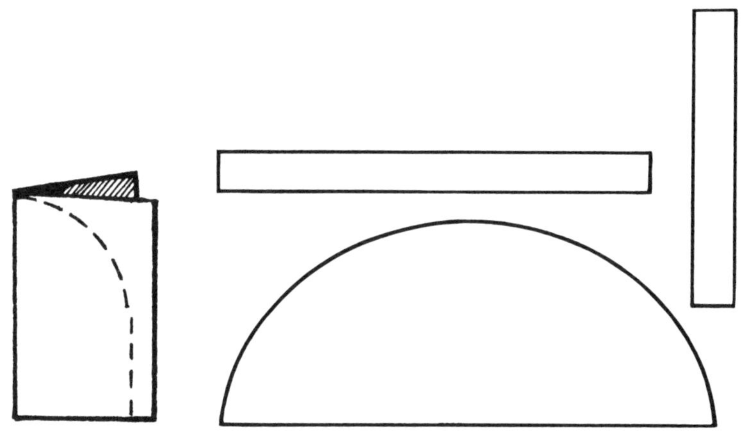

What You Need

Construction paper, black or brown and other colors
Pencil
Scissors
Glue

What You Do

1. Using the illustration on this page as a pattern, cut a half-circle and two rectangles from black paper.
2. Fold an 8" × 10" piece of black or brown construction paper in half. Then cut an arc to make an opening (see diagram). Unfold the paper and glue pieces of torn construction paper onto it.
3. Cut rectangles and a half-circle from black or brown paper.
4. Glue the rectangles to make a cross. Glue the cross and half-circle hill to the window-shaped arc.

More to Do

1. Cut shapes from green and brown paper, glue them to a lighter background, then write the words, "Jesus died for _______ (name of child)."
2. Glue the hill and cross onto marbled paper.
3. Tear colored tissue and glue it with a mixture of white glue and water.
4. Glue shapes inside an Easter egg-shaped oval.

The Lesson Connection

Jesus Died on the Cross: Matthew 27:45–54

Glue the stained glass window onto a larger sheet of paper and add the words of Jesus found in John 3:16. Read the words with the children to help them memorize the Bible verse. Invite them to show this picture and share these Bible words with others—maybe even someone who does not yet know that Jesus loves them.

Open Tomb

Shapes used: half-circle and triangle

What You Need

Construction paper
Pencil
Scissors
Glue

What You Do

1. Use the patterns on pages 5 and 23 to cut a large half-circle (Jesus' tomb) from gray construction paper, cut a small half-circle from its center to make a door. Cut a small gray circle to represent the stone rolled in front of the tomb door. Glue the two pieces to a sheet of construction paper.
2. Cut yellow triangles for rays of light and glue them around the tomb.

More to Do

1. Combine triangles and circles to add figures to the scene.
2. Glue black shapes onto marbled paper.
3. Add details and a Bible passage with markers or crayons.

The Lesson Connection

Jesus Is Alive: Luke 24:1–12

Have each child in your class make an Easter card to share the news of Jesus' resurrection with someone else. Fold a sheet of paper in half, glue the open tomb onto the front of the card, then write "Jesus Lives!" on the inside. As children work, read the Bible story and explain why it is still such an important story today. Remind the children that we still need a Savior, and that Jesus is the Way, the Truth, and the Life for all that would believe in Him. Sing an Easter praise song, such as "Do You Know Who Died for Me" or "Glory Be to Jesus."

Jesus Puppet

Shapes used: oval and rectangle

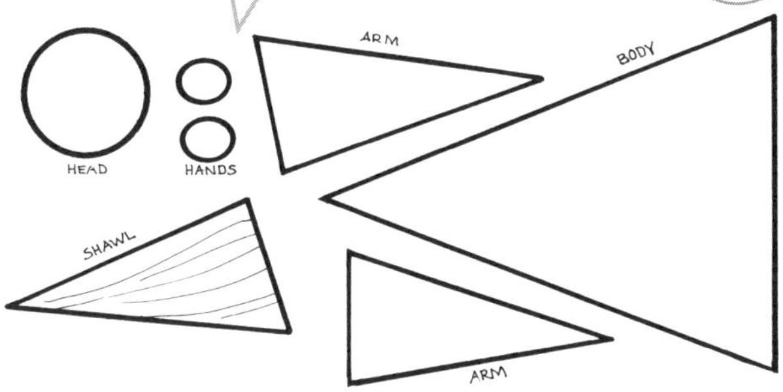

What You Need

Paper
Pencil
Scissors
Glue
Crayons or markers
Yarn
Tape
Craft stick

What You Do

1. Trace and cut the shapes given above.
2. Follow the diagram as you glue the shapes together to represent Jesus.
3. Use markers or crayons to add details.
4. Cut a piece of yarn and attach it to the back of the puppet. Tie the other end of the yarn to the craft stick and move the puppet as you tell stories about Jesus.

More to Do

1. Glue several circles or ovals together to represent a cloud and attach the other end of the yarn to it. Pull the figure of Jesus behind the cloud as you tell the story.
2. Glue the figure of Jesus onto a piece of paper. Add other figures to represent the disciples.
3. Fray a piece of brown yarn and glue it on for a beard.

The Lesson Connection

Jesus Goes Back to Heaven: Luke 24:50–53

Make a puppet representing Jesus. Read the story of Jesus' ascension into heaven, pulling up the puppet as you tell the story. Tell the children that before He went back to heaven, Jesus gave His disciples a very special job to do; we call it the Great Commission. Say that all of Jesus' followers, even young children, are part of the Great Commission and have a very important job to do: to tell others about Jesus as Savior.

Boat Puppet

Shapes used: triangle, half-oval, rectangle, circle

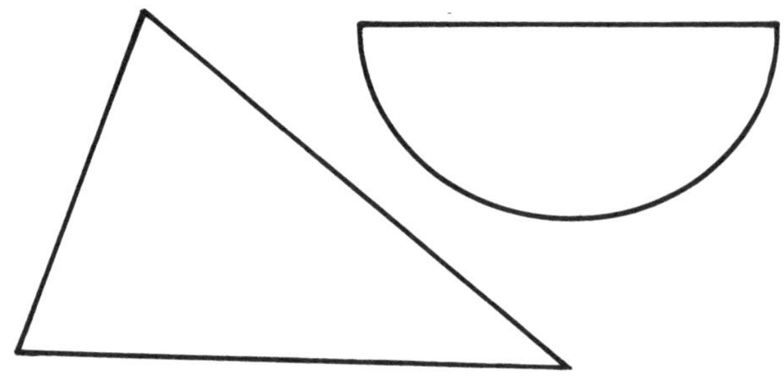

3. Glue the triangle to the top of the straw; leave a small space and glue the half-oval below it.
4. Draw faces on the gummed circles and attach them to the side of the boat.
5. Hold the bottom of the straw to move the boat.

More to Do

1. Glue the boat to a craft stick.
2. Cut a paper mast and glue the boat onto a piece of paper.
3. Cut circle faces from construction paper.
4. Glue circles to both sides of the boat. Draw the disciples during the storm on one side and after the storm on the other.

What You Need

Construction paper
Drinking straw
Gummed circles
Pencil
Scissors
Glue
Fine-tip marker

What You Do

1. Use the patterns for triangles and ovals.
2. Cut a brown half-oval for the boat and a white triangle for the sail.

The Lesson Connection

Jesus Stills the Storm: Mark 4:37–41

Use the puppet to tell the Bible story, moving it to illustrate the strength of the storm, and then suddenly stopping it after Jesus calmed the waves. Have each child make a boat to remind him or her of Jesus' power over the wind and waves. As they work, talk about how Jesus has the power to help us at all times and in any trouble. Say a prayer asking Jesus to protect and care for each child in the class. Name each child as you pray, or go around the classroom, asking each child to contribute a specific prayer thought or petition.

Fish

Shapes: oval and triangle

What You Need

Construction paper
Markers or crayons
Pencil
Scissors
Glue

What You Do

1. Use the oval and triangle on this page as a guide, or trace oval and triangle shapes found in your room.
2. Glue the triangle to one end of the oval to make a fish.
3. Use a marker or crayon to draw an eye and other desired markings on the fish.

More to Do

1. Have the children combine fish with the boat made on page 58 for a picture of the great catch of fishes.
2. Make the fish from craft foam or poster board. Staple or tape the fish to yarn to make a necklace.
3. Glue a circle to the top of a triangle to make a character. Use the character and fish to tell the story of Jonah and the big fish.

The Lesson Connection

The Early Christians: Acts 11:19–21

The fish symbol is often used by Christians to show others that they believe in Jesus as Savior. Explain to the children that the early Christians used to use the words "Jesus Christ, Son of God, Savior" to tell who Jesus is. They spoke Greek and took the first letter of each of these words to spell another word—fish. Sometimes they drew a picture of a fish to show they believed in Jesus. Ask children what words they might use to tell someone else who Jesus is. Have the children make a fish, then write the word "Jesus" on it. Send the fish home for them to put on their refrigerator or in a window to tell others they believe in Jesus.

Sunflower

Shapes used: circle, triangle, rectangle

What You Need

Small paper plate
Construction paper: yellow, green, and tan
Marker
Pencil
Scissors
Glue
Sunflower seeds (optional)

What You Do

1. Using a small triangle pattern, found on page 47, trace and cut enough yellow triangles to fit around the rim of the paper plate. Glue triangles in place.
2. Trace and cut a tan circle the size of the center of the paper plate; glue the circle onto the center of the plate.
3. Trace and glue on a green rectangular strip to the paper plate to represent a stem. Trace and cut two large triangles to glue on for leaves.
4. Draw a happy face or religious saying on the center of the sunflower.
5. Optional: Glue sunflower seeds on the center of the sunflower.

More to Do

1. Use a yellow paper plate, omit the tan center, and glue the seeds in the center of the plate.
2. Omit the paper plate and glue petals around a tan or yellow circle.
3. Cut petals from yellow ovals, cut one end of the ovals to a point.
4. Instead of drawing a happy face, glue on sunflower seeds to make a face.
5. Make a sunflower from a large paper plate. Use it as a mask and pretend you are a sunflower growing from a small seed into a tall flower. Sing "Oh, Who Can Make a Flower."

The Lesson Connection

God Cares for Flowers: Luke 12:27–31

Explain that Jesus once told His followers that God the Father, who takes care of the birds and flowers, also takes care of us. Have each child make a sunflower with a happy face. Glue sunflower seeds onto the lines to make the eyes, nose, and smile. As they work, talk about how God not only takes care of the sunflower but also uses its seeds to feed the birds to take care of them. Remind them that God thinks of everything and takes care of anything—His whole world and everything in it.

Thanksgiving Banner

Shapes used: half oval and circles

What You Need

Felt
Pencil or chalk
Scissors
Pencil
Craft glue
Dowel
Yarn

What You Do

1. Trace onto paper an oval pattern found on page 11. Cut it in half. Use the half-oval as a pattern. Use circle patterns or trace circles from round objects found in your classroom.
2. Trace and cut a felt bowl and felt circles representing fruit.
3. Glue the bowl onto a felt square. Glue circle shapes around the top of the bowl.
4. Cut two slits into the top of the felt rectangle; slip the dowel through it.
5. Tie a piece of yarn to each end of the dowel for hanging. Add glue to keep the yarn from slipping off the stick.

More to Do

1. Substitute paper for felt to make a Thanksgiving poster.
2. Cut shapes from fabric. Glue on fruit and outline with fabric paint.
3. Adapt ovals and circles to make different kinds of fruits.

The Lesson Connection

Be Thankful in all Circumstances: 1 Thessalonians 5:16

Explain to the children that we can be thankful all the time because God is our Creator and Provider—He never stops taking care of us. Use fabric paint or glitter glue to write the words "Give Thanks" onto the banner. As you work, talk about the many blessings that come to us from God the Father. Remember to include the blessing that God sent Jesus for the forgiveness of our sins.

Baptism Dove

Shapes used: oval, triangle, and rectangle

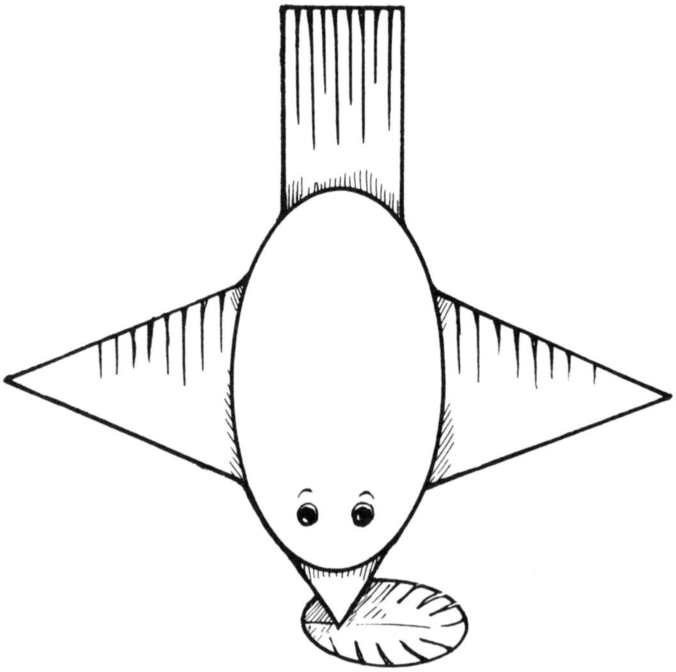

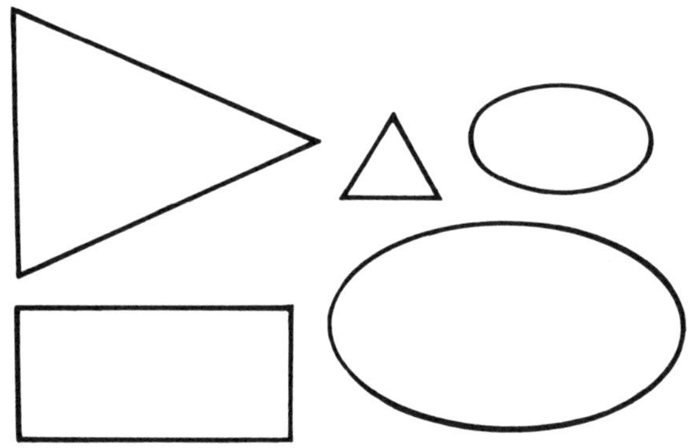

What You Need

Stiff white paper
Pencil
Scissors
Glue
Tape
White yarn

What You Do

1. Use the patterns on this page. If needed, enlarge them on a photocopier.
2. Copy and cut the following shapes from stiff white paper: one small and two large triangles, one rectangle, one oval.
3. Glue the pieces together as directed in the diagram.
4. Tape a piece of yarn to one side of the dove and hang it for a mobile.

More to Do

1. Cut dove from white poster board or decorative wrapping paper.
2. Use silver glitter glue for more details.
3. Omit rectangle tail and glue on white tail feathers instead.
4. Cut a green oval, fringe both sides, and glue it to the dove's beak.

The Lesson Connection

Jesus' Baptism: Matthew 3:13–17

Have each child make a mobile to illustrate how the Holy Spirit came down as a dove the day Jesus was baptized. Add each child's baptismal date or a baptismal Bible verse on one side of the dove. Remind the children that God welcomes us into His family and makes us His own through Baptism.

Trinity Plaque

Shapes used: triangle and circle

What You Need

Green and gold construction paper
Pencil
Scissors
Glue
Yarn
Hole punch

What You Do

1. Use the illustration above as a pattern guide. If needed, enlarge them on a photocopier.
2. Cut one green triangle and three gold rings.
3. Overlap the three circles and glue them together. Glue the circles onto the triangle. Use the diagram as a guide.
4. Punch a hole at the top of the triangle and tie yarn through the hole for a hanger.

More to Do

1. Cut shapes from craft foam; glue together with craft glue.
2. Cut circles from foil wrapping paper.
3. Omit triangle and combine circles only.

The Lesson Connection

Jesus' Baptism: Matthew 3:13–17

Each Person of the Trinity—Father, Son, Holy Ghost—was present at Jesus' Baptism. Have each child make a Trinity plaque to remind him or her of the God in whose name he or she was baptized. As children work, encourage them to talk about their own Baptism: who are their godparents? when were they baptized? how do they remember their Baptism? Send the plaque home as a reminder that through Baptism, God makes us His own for Jesus' sake.

Bible Story Index